C-588   CAREER EXAMINATION SERIES

This is your
PASSBOOK for...

Planner

Test Preparation Study Guide
Questions & Answers

NATIONAL LEARNING CORPORATION®

COPYRIGHT NOTICE

This book is SOLELY intended for, is sold ONLY to, and its use is RESTRICTED to individual, bona fide applicants or candidates who qualify by virtue of having seriously filed applications for appropriate license, certificate, professional and/or promotional advancement, higher school matriculation, scholarship, or other legitimate requirements of education and/or governmental authorities.

This book is NOT intended for use, class instruction, tutoring, training, duplication, copying, reprinting, excerption, or adaptation, etc., by:

1) Other publishers
2) Proprietors and/or Instructors of "Coaching" and/or Preparatory Courses
3) Personnel and/or Training Divisions of commercial, industrial, and governmental organizations
4) Schools, colleges, or universities and/or their departments and staffs, including teachers and other personnel
5) Testing Agencies or Bureaus
6) Study groups which seek by the purchase of a single volume to copy and/or duplicate and/or adapt this material for use by the group as a whole without having purchased individual volumes for each of the members of the group
7) Et al.

Such persons would be in violation of appropriate Federal and State statutes.

PROVISION OF LICENSING AGREEMENTS – Recognized educational, commercial, industrial, and governmental institutions and organizations, and others legitimately engaged in educational pursuits, including training, testing, and measurement activities, may address request for a licensing agreement to the copyright owners, who will determine whether, and under what conditions, including fees and charges, the materials in this book may be used them. In other words, a licensing facility exists for the legitimate use of the material in this book on other than an individual basis. However, it is asseverated and affirmed here that the material in this book CANNOT be used without the receipt of the express permission of such a licensing agreement from the Publishers. Inquiries re licensing should be addressed to the company, attention rights and permissions department.

All rights reserved, including the right of reproduction in whole or in part, in any form or by any means, electronic or mechanical, including photocopying, recording, or by any information storage and retrieval system, without permission in writing from the Publisher.

Copyright © 2024 by
National Learning Corporation

212 Michael Drive, Syosset, NY 11791
(516) 921-8888 • www.passbooks.com
E-mail: info@passbooks.com

PUBLISHED IN THE UNITED STATES OF AMERICA

PASSBOOK® SERIES

THE *PASSBOOK® SERIES* has been created to prepare applicants and candidates for the ultimate academic battlefield – the examination room.

At some time in our lives, each and every one of us may be required to take an examination – for validation, matriculation, admission, qualification, registration, certification, or licensure.

Based on the assumption that every applicant or candidate has met the basic formal educational standards, has taken the required number of courses, and read the necessary texts, the *PASSBOOK® SERIES* furnishes the one special preparation which may assure passing with confidence, instead of failing with insecurity. Examination questions – together with answers – are furnished as the basic vehicle for study so that the mysteries of the examination and its compounding difficulties may be eliminated or diminished by a sure method.

This book is meant to help you pass your examination provided that you qualify and are serious in your objective.

The entire field is reviewed through the huge store of content information which is succinctly presented through a provocative and challenging approach – the question-and-answer method.

A climate of success is established by furnishing the correct answers at the end of each test.

You soon learn to recognize types of questions, forms of questions, and patterns of questioning. You may even begin to anticipate expected outcomes.

You perceive that many questions are repeated or adapted so that you can gain acute insights, which may enable you to score many sure points.

You learn how to confront new questions, or types of questions, and to attack them confidently and work out the correct answers.

You note objectives and emphases, and recognize pitfalls and dangers, so that you may make positive educational adjustments.

Moreover, you are kept fully informed in relation to new concepts, methods, practices, and directions in the field.

You discover that you are actually taking the examination all the time: you are preparing for the examination by "taking" an examination, not by reading extraneous and/or supererogatory textbooks.

In short, this PASSBOOK®, used directedly, should be an important factor in helping you to pass your test.

PLANNER

DUTIES:
Participates in conducting land use and population studies, and in developing urban renewal plans, zoning ordinances, and land subdivision regulations; performs related duties as required.

SCOPE OF THE EXAMINATION:
The written test designed to evaluate knowledge, skills and or abilities in the following areas:
1. Computer-assisted mapping, including geographic information system (GIS) applications;
2. Collection, analysis, and presentation of data;
3. Sociological, economic, design and environmental factors involved in physical planning and community development;
4. Understanding and interpreting written material; and
5. Understanding and interpreting charts, graphs, maps and tabular material.

HOW TO TAKE A TEST

I. YOU MUST PASS AN EXAMINATION

A. WHAT EVERY CANDIDATE SHOULD KNOW

Examination applicants often ask us for help in preparing for the written test. What can I study in advance? What kinds of questions will be asked? How will the test be given? How will the papers be graded?

As an applicant for a civil service examination, you may be wondering about some of these things. Our purpose here is to suggest effective methods of advance study and to describe civil service examinations.

Your chances for success on this examination can be increased if you know how to prepare. Those "pre-examination jitters" can be reduced if you know what to expect. You can even experience an adventure in good citizenship if you know why civil service exams are given.

B. WHY ARE CIVIL SERVICE EXAMINATIONS GIVEN?

Civil service examinations are important to you in two ways. As a citizen, you want public jobs filled by employees who know how to do their work. As a job seeker, you want a fair chance to compete for that job on an equal footing with other candidates. The best-known means of accomplishing this two-fold goal is the competitive examination.

Exams are widely publicized throughout the nation. They may be administered for jobs in federal, state, city, municipal, town or village governments or agencies.

Any citizen may apply, with some limitations, such as the age or residence of applicants. Your experience and education may be reviewed to see whether you meet the requirements for the particular examination. When these requirements exist, they are reasonable and applied consistently to all applicants. Thus, a competitive examination may cause you some uneasiness now, but it is your privilege and safeguard.

C. HOW ARE CIVIL SERVICE EXAMS DEVELOPED?

Examinations are carefully written by trained technicians who are specialists in the field known as "psychological measurement," in consultation with recognized authorities in the field of work that the test will cover. These experts recommend the subject matter areas or skills to be tested; only those knowledges or skills important to your success on the job are included. The most reliable books and source materials available are used as references. Together, the experts and technicians judge the difficulty level of the questions.

Test technicians know how to phrase questions so that the problem is clearly stated. Their ethics do not permit "trick" or "catch" questions. Questions may have been tried out on sample groups, or subjected to statistical analysis, to determine their usefulness.

Written tests are often used in combination with performance tests, ratings of training and experience, and oral interviews. All of these measures combine to form the best-known means of finding the right person for the right job.

II. HOW TO PASS THE WRITTEN TEST

A. NATURE OF THE EXAMINATION

To prepare intelligently for civil service examinations, you should know how they differ from school examinations you have taken. In school you were assigned certain definite pages to read or subjects to cover. The examination questions were quite detailed and usually emphasized memory. Civil service exams, on the other hand, try to discover your present ability to perform the duties of a position, plus your potentiality to learn these duties. In other words, a civil service exam attempts to predict how successful you will be. Questions cover such a broad area that they cannot be as minute and detailed as school exam questions.

In the public service similar kinds of work, or positions, are grouped together in one "class." This process is known as *position-classification*. All the positions in a class are paid according to the salary range for that class. One class title covers all of these positions, and they are all tested by the same examination.

B. FOUR BASIC STEPS

1) Study the announcement

How, then, can you know what subjects to study? Our best answer is: "Learn as much as possible about the class of positions for which you've applied." The exam will test the knowledge, skills and abilities needed to do the work.

Your most valuable source of information about the position you want is the official exam announcement. This announcement lists the training and experience qualifications. Check these standards and apply only if you come reasonably close to meeting them.

The brief description of the position in the examination announcement offers some clues to the subjects which will be tested. Think about the job itself. Review the duties in your mind. Can you perform them, or are there some in which you are rusty? Fill in the blank spots in your preparation.

Many jurisdictions preview the written test in the exam announcement by including a section called "Knowledge and Abilities Required," "Scope of the Examination," or some similar heading. Here you will find out specifically what fields will be tested.

2) Review your own background

Once you learn in general what the position is all about, and what you need to know to do the work, ask yourself which subjects you already know fairly well and which need improvement. You may wonder whether to concentrate on improving your strong areas or on building some background in your fields of weakness. When the announcement has specified "some knowledge" or "considerable knowledge," or has used adjectives like "beginning principles of…" or "advanced … methods," you can get a clue as to the number and difficulty of questions to be asked in any given field. More questions, and hence broader coverage, would be included for those subjects which are more important in the work. Now weigh your strengths and weaknesses against the job requirements and prepare accordingly.

3) Determine the level of the position

Another way to tell how intensively you should prepare is to understand the level of the job for which you are applying. Is it the entering level? In other words, is this the position in which beginners in a field of work are hired? Or is it an intermediate or advanced level? Sometimes this is indicated by such words as "Junior" or "Senior" in the class title. Other jurisdictions use Roman numerals to designate the level – Clerk I, Clerk II, for example. The word "Supervisor" sometimes appears in the title. If the level is not indicated by the title, check the description of duties. Will you be working under very close supervision, or will you have responsibility for independent decisions in this work?

4) Choose appropriate study materials

Now that you know the subjects to be examined and the relative amount of each subject to be covered, you can choose suitable study materials. For beginning level jobs, or even advanced ones, if you have a pronounced weakness in some aspect of your training, read a modern, standard textbook in that field. Be sure it is up to date and has general coverage. Such books are normally available at your library, and the librarian will be glad to help you locate one. For entry-level positions, questions of appropriate difficulty are chosen – neither highly advanced questions, nor those too simple. Such questions require careful thought but not advanced training.

If the position for which you are applying is technical or advanced, you will read more advanced, specialized material. If you are already familiar with the basic principles of your field, elementary textbooks would waste your time. Concentrate on advanced textbooks and technical periodicals. Think through the concepts and review difficult problems in your field.

These are all general sources. You can get more ideas on your own initiative, following these leads. For example, training manuals and publications of the government agency which employs workers in your field can be useful, particularly for technical and professional positions. A letter or visit to the government department involved may result in more specific study suggestions, and certainly will provide you with a more definite idea of the exact nature of the position you are seeking.

III. KINDS OF TESTS

Tests are used for purposes other than measuring knowledge and ability to perform specified duties. For some positions, it is equally important to test ability to make adjustments to new situations or to profit from training. In others, basic mental abilities not dependent on information are essential. Questions which test these things may not appear as pertinent to the duties of the position as those which test for knowledge and information. Yet they are often highly important parts of a fair examination. For very general questions, it is almost impossible to help you direct your study efforts. What we can do is to point out some of the more common of these general abilities needed in public service positions and describe some typical questions.

1) General information

Broad, general information has been found useful for predicting job success in some kinds of work. This is tested in a variety of ways, from vocabulary lists to questions about current events. Basic background in some field of work, such as sociology or economics, may be sampled in a group of questions. Often these are principles which have become familiar to most persons through exposure rather than through formal training. It is difficult to advise you how to study for these questions; being alert to the world around you is our best suggestion.

2) Verbal ability

An example of an ability needed in many positions is verbal or language ability. Verbal ability is, in brief, the ability to use and understand words. Vocabulary and grammar tests are typical measures of this ability. Reading comprehension or paragraph interpretation questions are common in many kinds of civil service tests. You are given a paragraph of written material and asked to find its central meaning.

3) Numerical ability

Number skills can be tested by the familiar arithmetic problem, by checking paired lists of numbers to see which are alike and which are different, or by interpreting charts and graphs. In the latter test, a graph may be printed in the test booklet which you are asked to use as the basis for answering questions.

4) Observation

A popular test for law-enforcement positions is the observation test. A picture is shown to you for several minutes, then taken away. Questions about the picture test your ability to observe both details and larger elements.

5) Following directions

In many positions in the public service, the employee must be able to carry out written instructions dependably and accurately. You may be given a chart with several columns, each column listing a variety of information. The questions require you to carry out directions involving the information given in the chart.

6) Skills and aptitudes

Performance tests effectively measure some manual skills and aptitudes. When the skill is one in which you are trained, such as typing or shorthand, you can practice. These tests are often very much like those given in business school or high school courses. For many of the other skills and aptitudes, however, no short-time preparation can be made. Skills and abilities natural to you or that you have developed throughout your lifetime are being tested.

Many of the general questions just described provide all the data needed to answer the questions and ask you to use your reasoning ability to find the answers. Your best preparation for these tests, as well as for tests of facts and ideas, is to be at your physical and mental best. You, no doubt, have your own methods of getting into an exam-taking mood and keeping "in shape." The next section lists some ideas on this subject.

IV. KINDS OF QUESTIONS

Only rarely is the "essay" question, which you answer in narrative form, used in civil service tests. Civil service tests are usually of the short-answer type. Full instructions for answering these questions will be given to you at the examination. But in case this is your first experience with short-answer questions and separate answer sheets, here is what you need to know:

1) Multiple-choice Questions

Most popular of the short-answer questions is the "multiple choice" or "best answer" question. It can be used, for example, to test for factual knowledge, ability to solve problems or judgment in meeting situations found at work.

A multiple-choice question is normally one of three types—
- It can begin with an incomplete statement followed by several possible endings. You are to find the one ending which *best* completes the statement, although some of the others may not be entirely wrong.
- It can also be a complete statement in the form of a question which is answered by choosing one of the statements listed.

- It can be in the form of a problem – again you select the best answer.

Here is an example of a multiple-choice question with a discussion which should give you some clues as to the method for choosing the right answer:

When an employee has a complaint about his assignment, the action which will *best* help him overcome his difficulty is to
   A. discuss his difficulty with his coworkers
   B. take the problem to the head of the organization
   C. take the problem to the person who gave him the assignment
   D. say nothing to anyone about his complaint

In answering this question, you should study each of the choices to find which is best. Consider choice "A" – Certainly an employee may discuss his complaint with fellow employees, but no change or improvement can result, and the complaint remains unresolved. Choice "B" is a poor choice since the head of the organization probably does not know what assignment you have been given, and taking your problem to him is known as "going over the head" of the supervisor. The supervisor, or person who made the assignment, is the person who can clarify it or correct any injustice. Choice "C" is, therefore, correct. To say nothing, as in choice "D," is unwise. Supervisors have and interest in knowing the problems employees are facing, and the employee is seeking a solution to his problem.

2) True/False Questions

The "true/false" or "right/wrong" form of question is sometimes used. Here a complete statement is given. Your job is to decide whether the statement is right or wrong.

SAMPLE: A roaming cell-phone call to a nearby city costs less than a non-roaming call to a distant city.

This statement is wrong, or false, since roaming calls are more expensive.

This is not a complete list of all possible question forms, although most of the others are variations of these common types. You will always get complete directions for answering questions. Be sure you understand *how* to mark your answers – ask questions until you do.

V. RECORDING YOUR ANSWERS

Computer terminals are used more and more today for many different kinds of exams.
For an examination with very few applicants, you may be told to record your answers in the test booklet itself. Separate answer sheets are much more common. If this separate answer sheet is to be scored by machine – and this is often the case – it is highly important that you mark your answers correctly in order to get credit.
An electronic scoring machine is often used in civil service offices because of the speed with which papers can be scored. Machine-scored answer sheets must be marked with a pencil, which will be given to you. This pencil has a high graphite content which responds to the electronic scoring machine. As a matter of fact, stray dots may register as answers, so do not let your pencil rest on the answer sheet while you are pondering the correct answer. Also, if your pencil lead breaks or is otherwise defective, ask for another.

Since the answer sheet will be dropped in a slot in the scoring machine, be careful not to bend the corners or get the paper crumpled.

The answer sheet normally has five vertical columns of numbers, with 30 numbers to a column. These numbers correspond to the question numbers in your test booklet. After each number, going across the page are four or five pairs of dotted lines. These short dotted lines have small letters or numbers above them. The first two pairs may also have a "T" or "F" above the letters. This indicates that the first two pairs only are to be used if the questions are of the true-false type. If the questions are multiple choice, disregard the "T" and "F" and pay attention only to the small letters or numbers.

Answer your questions in the manner of the sample that follows:

32. The largest city in the United States is
   A. Washington, D.C.
   B. New York City
   C. Chicago
   D. Detroit
   E. San Francisco

1) Choose the answer you think is best. (New York City is the largest, so "B" is correct.)
2) Find the row of dotted lines numbered the same as the question you are answering. (Find row number 32)
3) Find the pair of dotted lines corresponding to the answer. (Find the pair of lines under the mark "B.")
4) Make a solid black mark between the dotted lines.

VI. BEFORE THE TEST

Common sense will help you find procedures to follow to get ready for an examination. Too many of us, however, overlook these sensible measures. Indeed, nervousness and fatigue have been found to be the most serious reasons why applicants fail to do their best on civil service tests. Here is a list of reminders:

- Begin your preparation early – Don't wait until the last minute to go scurrying around for books and materials or to find out what the position is all about.
- Prepare continuously – An hour a night for a week is better than an all-night cram session. This has been definitely established. What is more, a night a week for a month will return better dividends than crowding your study into a shorter period of time.
- Locate the place of the exam – You have been sent a notice telling you when and where to report for the examination. If the location is in a different town or otherwise unfamiliar to you, it would be well to inquire the best route and learn something about the building.
- Relax the night before the test – Allow your mind to rest. Do not study at all that night. Plan some mild recreation or diversion; then go to bed early and get a good night's sleep.
- Get up early enough to make a leisurely trip to the place for the test – This way unforeseen events, traffic snarls, unfamiliar buildings, etc. will not upset you.
- Dress comfortably – A written test is not a fashion show. You will be known by number and not by name, so wear something comfortable.

- Leave excess paraphernalia at home – Shopping bags and odd bundles will get in your way. You need bring only the items mentioned in the official notice you received; usually everything you need is provided. Do not bring reference books to the exam. They will only confuse those last minutes and be taken away from you when in the test room.
- Arrive somewhat ahead of time – If because of transportation schedules you must get there very early, bring a newspaper or magazine to take your mind off yourself while waiting.
- Locate the examination room – When you have found the proper room, you will be directed to the seat or part of the room where you will sit. Sometimes you are given a sheet of instructions to read while you are waiting. Do not fill out any forms until you are told to do so; just read them and be prepared.
- Relax and prepare to listen to the instructions
- If you have any physical problem that may keep you from doing your best, be sure to tell the test administrator. If you are sick or in poor health, you really cannot do your best on the exam. You can come back and take the test some other time.

VII. AT THE TEST

The day of the test is here and you have the test booklet in your hand. The temptation to get going is very strong. Caution! There is more to success than knowing the right answers. You must know how to identify your papers and understand variations in the type of short-answer question used in this particular examination. Follow these suggestions for maximum results from your efforts:

1) Cooperate with the monitor

The test administrator has a duty to create a situation in which you can be as much at ease as possible. He will give instructions, tell you when to begin, check to see that you are marking your answer sheet correctly, and so on. He is not there to guard you, although he will see that your competitors do not take unfair advantage. He wants to help you do your best.

2) Listen to all instructions

Don't jump the gun! Wait until you understand all directions. In most civil service tests you get more time than you need to answer the questions. So don't be in a hurry. Read each word of instructions until you clearly understand the meaning. Study the examples, listen to all announcements and follow directions. Ask questions if you do not understand what to do.

3) Identify your papers

Civil service exams are usually identified by number only. You will be assigned a number; you must not put your name on your test papers. Be sure to copy your number correctly. Since more than one exam may be given, copy your exact examination title.

4) Plan your time

Unless you are told that a test is a "speed" or "rate of work" test, speed itself is usually not important. Time enough to answer all the questions will be provided, but this does not mean that you have all day. An overall time limit has been set. Divide the total time (in minutes) by the number of questions to determine the approximate time you have for each question.

5) Do not linger over difficult questions

If you come across a difficult question, mark it with a paper clip (useful to have along) and come back to it when you have been through the booklet. One caution if you do this – be sure to skip a number on your answer sheet as well. Check often to be sure that you have not lost your place and that you are marking in the row numbered the same as the question you are answering.

6) Read the questions

Be sure you know what the question asks! Many capable people are unsuccessful because they failed to *read* the questions correctly.

7) Answer all questions

Unless you have been instructed that a penalty will be deducted for incorrect answers, it is better to guess than to omit a question.

8) Speed tests

It is often better NOT to guess on speed tests. It has been found that on timed tests people are tempted to spend the last few seconds before time is called in marking answers at random – without even reading them – in the hope of picking up a few extra points. To discourage this practice, the instructions may warn you that your score will be "corrected" for guessing. That is, a penalty will be applied. The incorrect answers will be deducted from the correct ones, or some other penalty formula will be used.

9) Review your answers

If you finish before time is called, go back to the questions you guessed or omitted to give them further thought. Review other answers if you have time.

10) Return your test materials

If you are ready to leave before others have finished or time is called, take ALL your materials to the monitor and leave quietly. Never take any test material with you. The monitor can discover whose papers are not complete, and taking a test booklet may be grounds for disqualification.

VIII. EXAMINATION TECHNIQUES

1) Read the general instructions carefully. These are usually printed on the first page of the exam booklet. As a rule, these instructions refer to the timing of the examination; the fact that you should not start work until the signal and must stop work at a signal, etc. If there are any *special* instructions, such as a choice of questions to be answered, make sure that you note this instruction carefully.

2) When you are ready to start work on the examination, that is as soon as the signal has been given, read the instructions to each question booklet, underline any key words or phrases, such as *least, best, outline, describe* and the like. In this way you will tend to answer as requested rather than discover on reviewing your paper that you *listed without describing*, that you selected the *worst* choice rather than the *best* choice, etc.

3) If the examination is of the objective or multiple-choice type – that is, each question will also give a series of possible answers: A, B, C or D, and you are called upon to select the best answer and write the letter next to that answer on your answer paper – it is advisable to start answering each question in turn. There may be anywhere from 50 to 100 such questions in the three or four hours allotted and you can see how much time would be taken if you read through all the questions before beginning to answer any. Furthermore, if you come across a question or group of questions which you know would be difficult to answer, it would undoubtedly affect your handling of all the other questions.

4) If the examination is of the essay type and contains but a few questions, it is a moot point as to whether you should read all the questions before starting to answer any one. Of course, if you are given a choice – say five out of seven and the like – then it is essential to read all the questions so you can eliminate the two that are most difficult. If, however, you are asked to answer all the questions, there may be danger in trying to answer the easiest one first because you may find that you will spend too much time on it. The best technique is to answer the first question, then proceed to the second, etc.

5) Time your answers. Before the exam begins, write down the time it started, then add the time allowed for the examination and write down the time it must be completed, then divide the time available somewhat as follows:
    - If 3-1/2 hours are allowed, that would be 210 minutes. If you have 80 objective-type questions, that would be an average of 2-1/2 minutes per question. Allow yourself no more than 2 minutes per question, or a total of 160 minutes, which will permit about 50 minutes to review.
    - If for the time allotment of 210 minutes there are 7 essay questions to answer, that would average about 30 minutes a question. Give yourself only 25 minutes per question so that you have about 35 minutes to review.

6) The most important instruction is to *read each question* and make sure you know what is wanted. The second most important instruction is to *time yourself properly* so that you answer every question. The third most important instruction is to *answer every question*. Guess if you have to but include something for each question. Remember that you will receive no credit for a blank and will probably receive some credit if you write something in answer to an essay question. If you guess a letter – say "B" for a multiple-choice question – you may have guessed right. If you leave a blank as an answer to a multiple-choice question, the examiners may respect your feelings but it will not add a point to your score. Some exams may penalize you for wrong answers, so in such cases *only*, you may not want to guess unless you have some basis for your answer.

7) Suggestions
    a. Objective-type questions
        1. Examine the question booklet for proper sequence of pages and questions
        2. Read all instructions carefully
        3. Skip any question which seems too difficult; return to it after all other questions have been answered
        4. Apportion your time properly; do not spend too much time on any single question or group of questions

5. Note and underline key words – *all, most, fewest, least, best, worst, same, opposite*, etc.
6. Pay particular attention to negatives
7. Note unusual option, e.g., unduly long, short, complex, different or similar in content to the body of the question
8. Observe the use of "hedging" words – *probably, may, most likely*, etc.
9. Make sure that your answer is put next to the same number as the question
10. Do not second-guess unless you have good reason to believe the second answer is definitely more correct
11. Cross out original answer if you decide another answer is more accurate; do not erase until you are ready to hand your paper in
12. Answer all questions; guess unless instructed otherwise
13. Leave time for review

  b. Essay questions
1. Read each question carefully
2. Determine exactly what is wanted. Underline key words or phrases.
3. Decide on outline or paragraph answer
4. Include many different points and elements unless asked to develop any one or two points or elements
5. Show impartiality by giving pros and cons unless directed to select one side only
6. Make and write down any assumptions you find necessary to answer the questions
7. Watch your English, grammar, punctuation and choice of words
8. Time your answers; don't crowd material

8) Answering the essay question

Most essay questions can be answered by framing the specific response around several key words or ideas. Here are a few such key words or ideas:

M's: manpower, materials, methods, money, management
P's: purpose, program, policy, plan, procedure, practice, problems, pitfalls, personnel, public relations

  a. Six basic steps in handling problems:
1. Preliminary plan and background development
2. Collect information, data and facts
3. Analyze and interpret information, data and facts
4. Analyze and develop solutions as well as make recommendations
5. Prepare report and sell recommendations
6. Install recommendations and follow up effectiveness

  b. Pitfalls to avoid
1. *Taking things for granted* – A statement of the situation does not necessarily imply that each of the elements is necessarily true; for example, a complaint may be invalid and biased so that all that can be taken for granted is that a complaint has been registered

2. *Considering only one side of a situation* – Wherever possible, indicate several alternatives and then point out the reasons you selected the best one
3. *Failing to indicate follow up* – Whenever your answer indicates action on your part, make certain that you will take proper follow-up action to see how successful your recommendations, procedures or actions turn out to be
4. *Taking too long in answering any single question* – Remember to time your answers properly

IX. AFTER THE TEST

Scoring procedures differ in detail among civil service jurisdictions although the general principles are the same. Whether the papers are hand-scored or graded by machine we have described, they are nearly always graded by number. That is, the person who marks the paper knows only the number – never the name – of the applicant. Not until all the papers have been graded will they be matched with names. If other tests, such as training and experience or oral interview ratings have been given, scores will be combined. Different parts of the examination usually have different weights. For example, the written test might count 60 percent of the final grade, and a rating of training and experience 40 percent. In many jurisdictions, veterans will have a certain number of points added to their grades.

After the final grade has been determined, the names are placed in grade order and an eligible list is established. There are various methods for resolving ties between those who get the same final grade – probably the most common is to place first the name of the person whose application was received first. Job offers are made from the eligible list in the order the names appear on it. You will be notified of your grade and your rank as soon as all these computations have been made. This will be done as rapidly as possible.

People who are found to meet the requirements in the announcement are called "eligibles." Their names are put on a list of eligible candidates. An eligible's chances of getting a job depend on how high he stands on this list and how fast agencies are filling jobs from the list.

When a job is to be filled from a list of eligibles, the agency asks for the names of people on the list of eligibles for that job. When the civil service commission receives this request, it sends to the agency the names of the three people highest on this list. Or, if the job to be filled has specialized requirements, the office sends the agency the names of the top three persons who meet these requirements from the general list.

The appointing officer makes a choice from among the three people whose names were sent to him. If the selected person accepts the appointment, the names of the others are put back on the list to be considered for future openings.

That is the rule in hiring from all kinds of eligible lists, whether they are for typist, carpenter, chemist, or something else. For every vacancy, the appointing officer has his choice of any one of the top three eligibles on the list. This explains why the person whose name is on top of the list sometimes does not get an appointment when some of the persons lower on the list do. If the appointing officer chooses the second or third eligible, the No. 1 eligible does not get a job at once, but stays on the list until he is appointed or the list is terminated.

X. HOW TO PASS THE INTERVIEW TEST

The examination for which you applied requires an oral interview test. You have already taken the written test and you are now being called for the interview test – the final part of the formal examination.

You may think that it is not possible to prepare for an interview test and that there are no procedures to follow during an interview. Our purpose is to point out some things you can do in advance that will help you and some good rules to follow and pitfalls to avoid while you are being interviewed.

What is an interview supposed to test?

The written examination is designed to test the technical knowledge and competence of the candidate; the oral is designed to evaluate intangible qualities, not readily measured otherwise, and to establish a list showing the relative fitness of each candidate – as measured against his competitors – for the position sought. Scoring is not on the basis of "right" and "wrong," but on a sliding scale of values ranging from "not passable" to "outstanding." As a matter of fact, it is possible to achieve a relatively low score without a single "incorrect" answer because of evident weakness in the qualities being measured.

Occasionally, an examination may consist entirely of an oral test – either an individual or a group oral. In such cases, information is sought concerning the technical knowledges and abilities of the candidate, since there has been no written examination for this purpose. More commonly, however, an oral test is used to supplement a written examination.

Who conducts interviews?

The composition of oral boards varies among different jurisdictions. In nearly all, a representative of the personnel department serves as chairman. One of the members of the board may be a representative of the department in which the candidate would work. In some cases, "outside experts" are used, and, frequently, a businessman or some other representative of the general public is asked to serve. Labor and management or other special groups may be represented. The aim is to secure the services of experts in the appropriate field.

However the board is composed, it is a good idea (and not at all improper or unethical) to ascertain in advance of the interview who the members are and what groups they represent. When you are introduced to them, you will have some idea of their backgrounds and interests, and at least you will not stutter and stammer over their names.

What should be done before the interview?

While knowledge about the board members is useful and takes some of the surprise element out of the interview, there is other preparation which is more substantive. It *is* possible to prepare for an oral interview – in several ways:

1) Keep a copy of your application and review it carefully before the interview

This may be the only document before the oral board, and the starting point of the interview. Know what education and experience you have listed there, and the sequence and dates of all of it. Sometimes the board will ask you to review the highlights of your experience for them; you should not have to hem and haw doing it.

2) Study the class specification and the examination announcement

Usually, the oral board has one or both of these to guide them. The qualities, characteristics or knowledges required by the position sought are stated in these documents. They offer valuable clues as to the nature of the oral interview. For example, if the job involves supervisory responsibilities, the announcement will usually indicate that knowledge of modern supervisory methods and the qualifications of the candidate as a supervisor will be tested. If so, you can expect such questions, frequently in the form of a hypothetical situation which you are expected to solve. NEVER go into an oral without knowledge of the duties and responsibilities of the job you seek.

3) Think through each qualification required
Try to visualize the kind of questions you would ask if you were a board member. How well could you answer them? Try especially to appraise your own knowledge and background in each area, *measured against the job sought*, and identify any areas in which you are weak. Be critical and realistic – do not flatter yourself.

4) Do some general reading in areas in which you feel you may be weak
For example, if the job involves supervision and your past experience has NOT, some general reading in supervisory methods and practices, particularly in the field of human relations, might be useful. Do NOT study agency procedures or detailed manuals. The oral board will be testing your understanding and capacity, not your memory.

5) Get a good night's sleep and watch your general health and mental attitude
You will want a clear head at the interview. Take care of a cold or any other minor ailment, and of course, no hangovers.

What should be done on the day of the interview?

Now comes the day of the interview itself. Give yourself plenty of time to get there. Plan to arrive somewhat ahead of the scheduled time, particularly if your appointment is in the fore part of the day. If a previous candidate fails to appear, the board might be ready for you a bit early. By early afternoon an oral board is almost invariably behind schedule if there are many candidates, and you may have to wait. Take along a book or magazine to read, or your application to review, but leave any extraneous material in the waiting room when you go in for your interview. In any event, relax and compose yourself.

The matter of dress is important. The board is forming impressions about you – from your experience, your manners, your attitude, and your appearance. Give your personal appearance careful attention. Dress your best, but not your flashiest. Choose conservative, appropriate clothing, and be sure it is immaculate. This is a business interview, and your appearance should indicate that you regard it as such. Besides, being well groomed and properly dressed will help boost your confidence.

Sooner or later, someone will call your name and escort you into the interview room. *This is it.* From here on you are on your own. It is too late for any more preparation. But remember, you asked for this opportunity to prove your fitness, and you are here because your request was granted.

What happens when you go in?

The usual sequence of events will be as follows: The clerk (who is often the board stenographer) will introduce you to the chairman of the oral board, who will introduce you to the other members of the board. Acknowledge the introductions before you sit down. Do not be surprised if you find a microphone facing you or a stenotypist sitting by. Oral interviews are usually recorded in the event of an appeal or other review.

Usually the chairman of the board will open the interview by reviewing the highlights of your education and work experience from your application – primarily for the benefit of the other members of the board, as well as to get the material into the record. Do not interrupt or comment unless there is an error or significant misinterpretation; if that is the case, do not hesitate. But do not quibble about insignificant matters. Also, he will usually ask you some question about your education, experience or your present job – partly to get you to start talking and to establish the interviewing "rapport." He may start the actual questioning, or turn it over to one of the other members. Frequently, each member undertakes the questioning on a particular area, one in which he is perhaps most competent, so you can expect each member to participate in the examination. Because time is limited, you may also expect some rather abrupt switches in the direction the questioning takes, so do not be upset by it. Normally, a board member will not pursue a single line of questioning unless he discovers a particular strength or weakness.

After each member has participated, the chairman will usually ask whether any member has any further questions, then will ask you if you have anything you wish to add. Unless you are expecting this question, it may floor you. Worse, it may start you off on an extended, extemporaneous speech. The board is not usually seeking more information. The question is principally to offer you a last opportunity to present further qualifications or to indicate that you have nothing to add. So, if you feel that a significant qualification or characteristic has been overlooked, it is proper to point it out in a sentence or so. Do not compliment the board on the thoroughness of their examination – they have been sketchy, and you know it. If you wish, merely say, "No thank you, I have nothing further to add." This is a point where you can "talk yourself out" of a good impression or fail to present an important bit of information. Remember, *you close the interview yourself*.

The chairman will then say, "That is all, Mr. _____, thank you." Do not be startled; the interview is over, and quicker than you think. Thank him, gather your belongings and take your leave. Save your sigh of relief for the other side of the door.

How to put your best foot forward

Throughout this entire process, you may feel that the board individually and collectively is trying to pierce your defenses, seek out your hidden weaknesses and embarrass and confuse you. Actually, this is not true. They are obliged to make an appraisal of your qualifications for the job you are seeking, and they want to see you in your best light. Remember, they must interview all candidates and a non-cooperative candidate may become a failure in spite of their best efforts to bring out his qualifications. Here are 15 suggestions that will help you:

1) **Be natural – Keep your attitude confident, not cocky**

If you are not confident that you can do the job, do not expect the board to be. Do not apologize for your weaknesses, try to bring out your strong points. The board is interested in a positive, not negative, presentation. Cockiness will antagonize any board member and make him wonder if you are covering up a weakness by a false show of strength.

2) **Get comfortable, but don't lounge or sprawl**

Sit erectly but not stiffly. A careless posture may lead the board to conclude that you are careless in other things, or at least that you are not impressed by the importance of the occasion. Either conclusion is natural, even if incorrect. Do not fuss with your clothing, a pencil or an ashtray. Your hands may occasionally be useful to emphasize a point; do not let them become a point of distraction.

3) **Do not wisecrack or make small talk**

This is a serious situation, and your attitude should show that you consider it as such. Further, the time of the board is limited – they do not want to waste it, and neither should you.

4) Do not exaggerate your experience or abilities

In the first place, from information in the application or other interviews and sources, the board may know more about you than you think. Secondly, you probably will not get away with it. An experienced board is rather adept at spotting such a situation, so do not take the chance.

5) If you know a board member, do not make a point of it, yet do not hide it

Certainly you are not fooling him, and probably not the other members of the board. Do not try to take advantage of your acquaintanceship – it will probably do you little good.

6) Do not dominate the interview

Let the board do that. They will give you the clues – do not assume that you have to do all the talking. Realize that the board has a number of questions to ask you, and do not try to take up all the interview time by showing off your extensive knowledge of the answer to the first one.

7) Be attentive

You only have 20 minutes or so, and you should keep your attention at its sharpest throughout. When a member is addressing a problem or question to you, give him your undivided attention. Address your reply principally to him, but do not exclude the other board members.

8) Do not interrupt

A board member may be stating a problem for you to analyze. He will ask you a question when the time comes. Let him state the problem, and wait for the question.

9) Make sure you understand the question

Do not try to answer until you are sure what the question is. If it is not clear, restate it in your own words or ask the board member to clarify it for you. However, do not haggle about minor elements.

10) Reply promptly but not hastily

A common entry on oral board rating sheets is "candidate responded readily," or "candidate hesitated in replies." Respond as promptly and quickly as you can, but do not jump to a hasty, ill-considered answer.

11) Do not be peremptory in your answers

A brief answer is proper – but do not fire your answer back. That is a losing game from your point of view. The board member can probably ask questions much faster than you can answer them.

12) Do not try to create the answer you think the board member wants

He is interested in what kind of mind you have and how it works – not in playing games. Furthermore, he can usually spot this practice and will actually grade you down on it.

13) Do not switch sides in your reply merely to agree with a board member

Frequently, a member will take a contrary position merely to draw you out and to see if you are willing and able to defend your point of view. Do not start a debate, yet do not surrender a good position. If a position is worth taking, it is worth defending.

14) Do not be afraid to admit an error in judgment if you are shown to be wrong

The board knows that you are forced to reply without any opportunity for careful consideration. Your answer may be demonstrably wrong. If so, admit it and get on with the interview.

15) Do not dwell at length on your present job

The opening question may relate to your present assignment. Answer the question but do not go into an extended discussion. You are being examined for a *new* job, not your present one. As a matter of fact, try to phrase ALL your answers in terms of the job for which you are being examined.

Basis of Rating

Probably you will forget most of these "do's" and "don'ts" when you walk into the oral interview room. Even remembering them all will not ensure you a passing grade. Perhaps you did not have the qualifications in the first place. But remembering them will help you to put your best foot forward, without treading on the toes of the board members.

Rumor and popular opinion to the contrary notwithstanding, an oral board wants you to make the best appearance possible. They know you are under pressure – but they also want to see how you respond to it as a guide to what your reaction would be under the pressures of the job you seek. They will be influenced by the degree of poise you display, the personal traits you show and the manner in which you respond.

ABOUT THIS BOOK

This book contains tests divided into Examination Sections. Go through each test, answering every question in the margin. We have also attached a sample answer sheet at the back of the book that can be removed and used. At the end of each test look at the answer key and check your answers. On the ones you got wrong, look at the right answer choice and learn. Do not fill in the answers first. Do not memorize the questions and answers, but understand the answer and principles involved. On your test, the questions will likely be different from the samples. Questions are changed and new ones added. If you understand these past questions you should have success with any changes that arise. Tests may consist of several types of questions. We have additional books on each subject should more study be advisable or necessary for you. Finally, the more you study, the better prepared you will be. This book is intended to be the last thing you study before you walk into the examination room. Prior study of relevant texts is also recommended. NLC publishes some of these in our Fundamental Series. Knowledge and good sense are important factors in passing your exam. Good luck also helps. So now study this Passbook, absorb the material contained within and take that knowledge into the examination. Then do your best to pass that exam.

EXAMINATION SECTION

EXAMINATION SECTION
TEST 1

DIRECTIONS: Each question or incomplete statement is followed by several suggested answers of completions. Select the one that BEST answers the question or complete the statement. PRINT THE LETTER OF THE CORRECT ANSWER IN THE SPACE AT THE RIGHT.

1. Geographic information is
    A. linear
    B. one-dimensional
    C. multi-dimensional
    D. none of the above

    1._____

2. GIS is an abbreviation of
    A. Global Integration System
    B. Global Information System
    C. Geographic Information Standards
    D. Geographic Information System

    2._____

3. Two main data types in GIS are
    A. images and graphics
    B. vector and maps
    C. vector and raster
    D. latitude and longitude

    3._____

4. Vector data consists of:
    A. land maps and images
    B. satellite images
    C. postal codes, latitude and longitude
    D. points, lines and polygons

    4._____

5. Three stages of executing GIS are
    A. taking, uploading and viewing images
    B. latitudes, longitudes and postal codes
    C. data preparation, analysis and presentation
    D. data, information and knowledge

    5._____

6. GPS is an abbreviation of
    A. Geographic Positioning System
    B. Global Positioning Standard
    C. Geographic Planning System
    D. Global Positioning System

    6._____

7. A map is a
    A. database of locations
    B. set of geographic images
    C. miniature representation of some part of the real world
    D. grid of values

    7._____

1

8. The database used for GIS is called
   A. Spatial Database
   B. General Database
   C. Map Database
   D. Positioning Database

9. GIS is a system capable of
   A. storing and displaying an individual's bio-data
   B. storing, displaying and manipulating data related to space
   C. assembling, storing, manipulating and displaying geographically referenced information
   D. assembling, storing, manipulating and displaying environmentally referenced data

10. Decreasing the map scale would
    A. show more detail
    B. show less detail
    C. would not have any effect
    D. none of the above

11. Data is geo-referenced when it is
    A. tagged
    B. analyzed
    C. associated with a position using spatial reference system
    D. retrieved

12. Geo-coding is the process of
    A. writing any program for GIS
    B. finding associated geographic coordinates of data
    C. encrypting location data
    D. viewing data on maps

13. Raster data consists of
    A. location information
    B. data tables
    C. a sorted grid of different values making up an image
    D. vegetation and land maps

14. Which of the following is NOT a component of a geodatabase?
    A. Relationship classes
    B. Shapefile
    C. Geographic features
    D. Attribute data

15. COGO data entry refers to
    A. entering data by using coordinate geometery
    B. entering data by using coordinal geography
    C. software for data entry
    D. none of the above

16. The relationship between the directions on the map and the corresponding compass directions is called
    A. map scale
    B. orientation of a map
    C. GPS
    D. COGO

17. The process of converting geographic features on an analog map into digital format is known as map _____.
    A. orientation
    B. organization
    C. digitization
    D. conversion

18. The data format DRG is an acronym of
    A. Digital Reclassification Graphics
    B. Digital Record Graphics
    C. Digital Raster Graphics
    D. Documented Record Graphics

19. DOQ is used in GIS when a map shows
    A. topographic map
    B. base map
    C. aerial photography
    D. polygons

20. Which of the following is NOT a type of attribute data?
    A. BLOB
    B. Date
    C. Integer
    D. OLE

21. _____ is known as the father of GIS.
    A. John Snow
    B. Howard T. Fisher
    C. ESRI
    D. Dr. Roger Tomlinson

22. GeoRSS refers to
    A. geographic images
    B. raster data file
    C. standard for encoding location as part of a web feed
    D. standard for decoding the location into non-spatial formats

23. XML notation for expressing geographic annotation is called
    A. GML
    B. KML
    C. Shape file
    D. XGML

24. TIGER file format is an example of
    A. raster data
    B. topographic map
    C. vector data
    D. non-spatial data

25. A set of reference points on the Earth's surface against which position measurements are made is known as
    A. COGO
    B. geodetic datum
    C. map base
    D. map reference

KEY (CORRECT ANSWERS)

1.	C	11.	C
2.	D	12.	B
3.	C	13.	C
4.	D	14.	A
5.	C	15.	A
6.	D	16.	B
7.	C	17.	C
8.	A	18.	C
9.	C	19.	C
10.	B	20.	D
21.	D		
22.	C		
23.	B		
24.	C		
25.	B		

TEST 2

DIRECTIONS: Each question or incomplete statement is followed by several suggested answers of completions. Select the one that BEST answers the question or complete the statement. PRINT THE LETTER OF THE CORRECT ANSWER IN THE SPACE AT THE RIGHT.

1. Which one of the following is NOT an example of spatial data? 1._____
    A. Lines and Polygons
    B. Points showing locations
    C. Satellite images
    D. Times of specific events

2. Cartography is defined as 2._____
    A. storing location data
    B. an art of drawing maps
    C. storing data in a cart
    D. retrieving location data

3. Acquisition of information without making physical contact is known as 3._____
    A. GIS
    B. remote sensing
    C. virtual information
    D. GPS

4. Pixel size is measure of 4._____
    A. map distance
    B. polygons
    C. spatial resolution
    D. GPS

5. Aligning geographic data to a known coordinate system is called 5._____
    A. geo-coding
    B. geo-caching
    C. GPS
    D. geo-referencing

6. Web environments allowing access to geo-spatial information are called 6._____
    A. GIS servers
    B. web-GIS clients
    C. spatial databases
    D. none of the above

7. A photograph of earth's surface taken from an object flying above is called a(n) 7._____
    A. geo-photograph
    B. aerial photograph
    C. still photograph
    D. GIS image

8. Process of converting raster data into vector data is known as
   A. rasterization
   B. vectorization
   C. geo-conversion
   D. none of the above

9. Two types of geographic data fields are
   A. vector and raster
   B. long and short
   C. discrete and continuous
   D. latitude and longitude

10. A base map is
    A. a map of a base camp
    B. a basic map
    C. any map containing geographic features for geographical reference
    D. none of the above

11. Secondary sources of GIS data are
    A. sources collected in digital format
    B. digital and analog datasets originally captured for another purpose and have to be converted in proper format
    C. datasets collected from web as shape file
    D. GIS datasets that are captured without human physical contact

12. A survey that provides information about relative locations and features of land is called a _____ survey.
    A. land
    B. topographic
    C. population
    D. geo-

13. Geo-coding service is used for
    A. converting spatial data into descriptive addresses
    B. converting non-spatial descriptions of places into spatial data
    C. conversion of analog map into digital
    D. coding for GIS

14. The process of adding geographical metadata to different media is known as geo-_____.
    A. tagging
    B. coding
    C. fencing
    D. tracking

15. An attribute table consists of
    A. address codes
    B. personality attributes
    C. values representing geographic features
    D. values showing map projections

16. Which of the following has a single attribute assigned to each cell in the raster that defines which c category the cell belongs to? 16.____
    A. Continuous raster data
    B. Discrete raster data
    C. Integer raster data
    D. Continuous vector data

17. ArcGIS refers to 17.____
    A. a standard protocol for serving geo-referenced map images over the Internet
    B. a platform for designing and managing solutions through application of geographic knowledge
    C. satellite imagery for geographic analysis
    D. GPS simulation tool

18. OpenStreetMap is an example of _____ web maps. 18.____
    A. personalized
    B. distributed
    C. collaborative
    D. user

19. A standard protocol for serving geo-referenced map images over the Internet is 19.____
    A. ArcGIS
    B. Web Map Service
    C. Web Map Client
    D. Map protocol

20. Coordinate transformation between two vector spaces in GIS is done through 20.____
    A. angle transformation
    B. affine transformation
    C. image transformation
    D. position transformation

21. Information needed for a GPS receiver to calculate the position downloaded from satellite every day is called _____ data. 21.____
    A. almanac
    B. affine
    C. ephemeris
    D. raster

22. Nearest Neighbor method is an example of 22.____
    A. geo-statistical interpolation
    B. non-geostatistical interpolation
    C. geographic interpolator
    D. univariate interpolator

23. In GPS, a file transmitted from a satellite to a receiver that contains information about precise orbits of all satellites is known as _____ data. 23.____
    A. vector
    B. almanac
    C. ephemeris
    D. affinity

24. The method to determine the origins of the value of a continuous attribute is
    A. interpolation
    B. Nearest Neighbor
    C. Factorial Kriging
    D. Block Kriging

25. The geo-database of ArcGIS uses _____ database.
    A. relational
    B. object relational
    C. simple
    D. multi-dimensional

KEY (CORRECT ANSWERS)

1. D
2. B
3. B
4. C
5. D

6. B
7. B
8. B
9. C
10. C

11. B
12. B
13. B
14. A
15. C

16. B
17. B
18. C
19. B
20. B

21. A
22. A
23. C
24. C
25. B

TEST 3

DIRECTIONS: Each question or incomplete statement is followed by several suggested answers of completions. Select the one that BEST answers the question or complete the statement. PRINT THE LETTER OF THE CORRECT ANSWER IN THE SPACE AT THE RIGHT.

1. Google Places API is used for 1._____
   A. searching points of interest
   B. geocoding
   C. tracking path
   D. finding directions

2. Location analytics refers to 2._____
   A. analyzing location statistics
   B. analyzing population with reference to geography
   C. analyzing data of land
   D. adding a geographic dimension to business analytics

3. Which of the following geographic information would NOT be found by involving GIS? 3._____
   A. Knowing criminal activities in a particular area
   B. Knowing how much land area in Pakistan has been urbanized
   C. Estimating the population of Pakistan in 2015
   D. Determining the number of health facilities in a particular area

4. Two basic types of map information in GIS are 4._____
   A. spatial and non-spatial
   B. geographic and personal
   C. spatial and personal
   D. attribute and non-attribute

5. The art of surveying the earth's surface considering its shape and size is known as 5._____
   A. Earth survey
   B. geographic survey
   C. geodetic survey
   D. geomapping

6. In cartography, any network of parallel and perpendicular lines superimposed on a map for reference is called 6._____
   A. shape file   C. matrix
   B. grid   D. geo-reference

7. The intersection of x and y axis in the map projected coordinate system refers to 7._____
   A. point in east direction
   B. point in Equator
   C. origin of the location
   D. none of the above

8. Google Maps Image API allows
   A. embedding a static Google Maps image into web page
   B. creating a gallery of maps
   C. map colorization
   D. map simulation

9. The procedure for estimating the value of properties at unsampled locations is called
   A. geographic estimation
   B. spatial Interpolation
   C. spatial sampling
   D. location estimation

10. ESRI product that integrates traditional GIS with cloud platform is
    A. EsriCloud
    B. ArcGIS Online
    C. ArcGIS server
    D. ArcView

11. Which of the following is not a GIS package?
    A. QGIS   C. NetScape
    B. ArcGIS   D. Idrisi32

12. AM/FM GIS refers to
    A. GIS tools that allow users to digitize, manage and analyze land record data
    B. GIS software that allows utility users to digitize, manage and analyze their utility network data
    C. GIS software that allows users to digitize, manage and analyze population data
    D. none of the above

13. Which of the following is a true statement?
    A. Vector data resolution has to be enhanced for viewing it properly
    B. Vector data topology is dynamic
    C. Vector data can be represented in its original resolution
    D. Continuous data is represented very effectively in vector format

14. Digital Elevation Model (DEM) represents a
    A. terrain surface in 3D
    B. shapefile
    C. TIGER format
    D. water surface

15. Which one of the following is an example of coverage data in GIS?
    A. Shape file
    B. Geospatial database
    C. Raster
    D. Vector

16. Transformation of Earth's model from 3D to 2D is known as
    A. map projection
    B. map conversion
    C. cartography
    D. elevation

17. What is E00 file?
    A. A file containing latitudes and longitudes of different landscapes
    B. A file containing locations of different points of interest in the world
    C. A Google Maps data file
    D. ESRI's file format to import and export ArcInfo data files

18. TIGER is an abbreviation of
    A. Topological Intelligence and Geographic Environment and Referencing
    B. Topologically Integrated Geographic Environment and Referencing
    C. Topologically Integrated Geographic Encoding and Referencing
    D. Topologically Integrated Geo-spatial Environment and Referencing

19. TIGER format was previously known as
    A. DIME
    B. DIVE
    C. E00
    D. Shapefile

20. GRASS is a GIS tool that stands for
    A. Geographic Resources Almanac Support System
    B. Geo-spatial Review Analysis Support System
    C. Geographic Resources Analysis Support System
    D. Geographic Resources Alternate Simple System

21. A vector based representation of physical land made up of irregularly distributed nodes and lines with 3D coordinates is known as
    A. Digital Elevation Model
    B. Triangulated Irregular Network
    C. Continuous data
    D. TIGER

22. A grid-based GIS coordinate system that specifies locations on Earth's surface is called
    A. Universal Transverse Mercator (UTM)
    B. North American Datum (NAD)
    C. map projection
    D. tessellation

23. A Digital Earth Reference Model (DERM) refers to a
    A. geospatial platform that acts as a reference model to use geo-referenced information
    B. geospatial framework that allows importing and exporting of vector data
    C. simulation of earth's surface in 3D
    D. none of the above

24. In GIS, coverage refers to
    A. mapping of multiple aspects in a single representation
    B. mapping of one aspect of data in space
    C. types of data in a system
    D. none of the above

25. GeoTIFF is a file format that
    A. embeds geo-coded information into raster file
    B. embeds image registration information directory into raster file
    C. embeds geo-coded information into vector file
    D. imports or exports geo-spatial data

KEY (CORRECT ANSWERS)

1. A
2. D
3. C
4. A
5. C

6. B
7. C
8. A
9. B
10. B

11. C
12. B
13. C
14. A
15. A

16. A
17. D
18. C
19. A
20. C

21. B
22. A
23. A
24. B
25. B

TEST 4

DIRECTIONS: Each question or incomplete statement is followed by several suggested answers of completions. Select the one that BEST answers the question or complete the statement. PRINT THE LETTER OF THE CORRECT ANSWER IN THE SPACE AT THE RIGHT.

1. Google Directions API refers to a(n) 1._____
    A. service that directs and helps in map usage
    B. API used to return distance between origin and destination
    C. service that calculates directions between locations
    D. API to follow location of a particular user

2. Which form of representation does a paper map use? 2._____
    A. Analogue
    B. Binary
    C. Decimal
    D. Digital

3. Which of the following statements are true? 3._____
    A. GISs are incapable of getting field data into their databases
    B. GISs are incapable of getting satellite imagery into their databases
    C. GISs are incapable of getting attribute data into their databases
    D. GISs are incapable of storing all types of map data in the ordinary flat file structure

4. Data about data is called 4._____
    A. nested data
    B. meta data
    C. world wide web
    D. catalog

5. A digitizing tablet and mouse are examples of 5._____
    A. infrastructure of GIS
    B. input devices used in digitizing
    C. output devices used in digitizing
    D. techniques of digitizing

6. The origin of a raster grid in IDRISI is 6._____
    A. lower right corner
    B. upper right corner
    C. upper left corner
    D. random

7. To embed a Google Map on a web page without any JavaScript or page loading, which of the following APIs can be used? 7._____
    A. Street View API
    B. Google Maps Image API
    C. Google Places API
    D. Static Maps API

8. The division of a two-dimensional area into polygonal tiles, or a three-dimensional area into polyhedral blocks, is known as
   A. projection
   B. tessellation
   C. interpolation
   D. alleviation

   8._____

9. A federally mandated framework of spatial data that refers to U.S is known as
   A. National Spatial Data Infrastructure (NSDI)
   B. North American Datum (NAD)
   C. American National Standards Institute (ANSI)
   D. Environmental Systems Research Institute (ESRI)

   9._____

10. Batch geo-coding refers to the process of geo-coding
    A. one address at a time
    B. multiple address at a time
    C. addresses in Google Maps API
    D. addresses in standard format

    10._____

11. The process of determining exact position with GPS and recording location of an object at regular intervals as well as allowing the location to show on map is known as
    A. geo-tagging
    B. geo-coding
    C. geo-caching
    D. geo-tracking

    11._____

12. Controlling of advertisements within maps is done with the help of
    A. Google Places API
    B. Google Maps API for Business
    C. Google Maps Web Services
    D. Google Directions API

    12._____

13. A Google Maps API responsible for returning distance based on recommended route between start and end point is known as
    A. Google Distance Matrix API
    B. Google Distance Calculation API
    C. Google Directions API
    D. Google Elevation API

    13._____

14. If we want to determine the depth locations of an ocean floor, we'll use which of the following APIs?
    A. Google Directions API
    B. Google Distance Matrix API
    C. Google Elevation API
    D. Google Places API

    14._____

15. Google Street View Image API allows
    A. embedding a static StreetView Panorama on our web page
    B. embedding a dynamic StreetView Panorama using JavaScript
    C. showing simulation of StreetView Panorama
    D. none of the above

    15._____

16. To overlay, compare or cross-analyze two maps in a GIS, both maps must be   16._____
    A. in digital form
    B. in the same map projection
    C. at the same equivalent scale
    D. on the same coordinate system

17. In GIS, property of connectivity is also known as   17._____
    A. proximity
    B. neighborhood
    C. topology
    D. boolean identity

18. Using a smaller cell size in a raster GIS will result in   18._____
    A. more storage required
    B. less storage required
    C. a greater range of values
    D. less resolution

19. Examples of points, lines and areas in context of GIS data are   19._____
    A. wetlands, ponds and parks
    B. oil wells, pipelines and fields
    C. trees, loggers and lumber mills
    D. GPS points, big businesses and land covers

20. Which of the following types of remote sensing would be best suited for locating deforestation?   20._____
    A. Thermal infrared
    B. Microwave
    C. Radar
    D. Color infrared

21. Three models that have been used by geodesy and cartography are   21._____
    A. ellipsoid, sphere and geoid
    B. circle, cone and cylinder
    C. ellipsoid, spheroid and geode
    D. prolate spheroid, oblate cylindroid and geoid

22. An oblate ellipsoid is a(n)   22._____
    A. circle rotated about its major axis
    B. ellipse rotated about its shorter axis
    C. map projection
    D. ellipse rotated about its longer axis

23. Which is NOT true of the UTM system?   23._____
    A. The earth is divided into 60 UTM zones, 6 degrees wide
    B. Zones are numbered west to east, starting at 180 degrees west
    C. Each zone is drawn on a Transverse Mercator projection, centered on the central meridian
    D. The UTM system covers the whole planet in one consistent metric system of coordinates

24. Tobler's first law of geography states that
    A. any area of interest will always lie at the intersection of at least two maps or images
    B. everything is related to everything else, but near things are more related than distant things
    C. resolution of raster data is directly related to cell size
    D. none of the above

    24._____

25. Web Map Server Configuration refers to
    A. GIS tool
    B. a set of interface specifications that provides uniform access by Web clients to maps rendered by map servers on the Internet
    C. network protocols
    D. none of the above

    25._____

KEY (CORRECT ANSWERS)

1.	C		11.	D
2.	A		12.	B
3.	D		13.	A
4.	B		14.	C
5.	B		15.	A
6.	C		16.	A
7.	D		17.	C
8.	B		18.	A
9.	A		19.	B
10.	B		20.	D

21.	C
22.	B
23.	D
24.	B
25.	B

EXAMINATION SECTION
TEST 1

DIRECTIONS: Each question or incomplete statement is followed by several suggested answers or completions. Select the one that BEST answers the question or completes the statement. *PRINT THE LETTER OF THE CORRECT ANSWER IN THE SPACE AT THE RIGHT.*

1. The scale of one inch equals one hundred feet is equivalent to the fraction 1.____

    A. 1/100 B. 100/1 C. 1200/1 D. 1/1200

2. The predominant type of imaging used for civil engineering applications is the traditional _____ centimeter format frame aerial photograph. 2.____

    A. 19 x 19 B. 21 x 21 C. 23 x 23 D. 25 x 25

3. Both photogrammetry and remote sensing in the past relied on photographs that are 3.____

    A. silver borate emulsion products
    B. silver halide emulsion products
    C. ammonium cyanide emulsion products
    D. silver chlorate emulsion products

4. $5\,\mu m$ is equal to five _____ of a meter. 4.____

    A. ten thousandth B. hundred thousandth
    C. millionth D. ten millionth

5. Raw aerial photographs should not be used as a map because of image tilt and 5.____

    A. inability to determine the scale of the map with sufficient accuracy
    B. blurred images
    C. parallax
    D. terrain relief

6. If f is the focal length of an aerial camera and H is the height of the airplane above the ground, the scale of the photograph is equal to 6.____

    A. f/H+f B. f/H-f C. f/H D. H-f/H+f

7. Of the following statements related to the shape of the earth, the one that is CORRECT is: 7.____

    A. A plane through the poles will intersect the surface of the earth in a circle while a plane through the equator will intersect the earth in an ellipse.
    B. A plane through the poles will intersect the surface of the earth in an ellipse while a plane through the equator will intersect the surface of the earth in a circle.
    C. A plane through the poles will intersect the surface of the earth in a circle while a plane through the equator will intersect the surface of the earth in a circle.
    D. A plane through the poles will intersect the surface of the earth in an ellipse while a plane through the equator will intersect the surface of the earth in an ellipse.

8. The latitude of New York City is MOST NEARLY   8.____

   A. 36°-45'N   B. 38°-45'N   C. 40°-45'N   D. 42°-45'N

9. The azimuth of a line is its direction as given by the angle between the meridian and the   9.____
   line measured in a

   A. clockwise direction usually from the south branch of the meridian
   B. counterclockwise direction usually from the south branch of the meridian
   C. clockwise direction usually from the north branch of the meridian
   D. counterclockwise direction usually from the north branch of the meridian

10. A geometric map projection in which the projection surface is a plane tangent to the   10.____
    sphere at any point and the point used as a projection center is the center of the sphere
    is a(n) _____ projection.

    A. stereographic   B. gnomonic
    C. orthographic   D. equal area

11. A map projection showing the correct angle between any pair of intersecting lines mak-   11.____
    ing small areas that seems to have a correct shape is known as _____ projection.

    A. conformal   B. isoclinic
    C. isometric   D. axonometric

12. The projection on which circles on the earth will appear as circles on the map is a(n)   12.____
    _____ projection.

    A. isometric   B. orthographic
    C. gnomonic   D. stereographic

13. An orthographic projection whose projection surface is a plane tangent to the sphere has   13.____
    its projection center at

    A. the center of the sphere
    B. the end of the diameter opposite to the point of tangency
    C. an infinite distance from the plane
    D. a variable distance from the plane

14. The *disadvantage* of the Mercator projection is that   14.____

    A. a line of constant bearing is a straight line on the map
    B. areas are distorted in size
    C. the scale at the equator is never accurate
    D. the meridians are not parallel on the map

15. An advantage of geographic coordinates is that it   15.____

    A. is more accurate than any other system
    B. is easier to determine than any other system
    C. has universal recognition
    D. can be determined by astronomical surveying

16. The conic projection with two standard parallels is known as the _____ conformal projector. 16._____

    A. Mercator
    B. Albers
    C. Transverse Mercator
    D. Lambert

17. The conic projection with two standard parallels is used for the plane coordinate system for states 17._____

    A. having conical shapes
    B. that are nearly square shaped
    C. that have greater north-south than east-west extent
    D. that have greater east-west than north-south extent

18. The Mercator projection is a projection on a cylinder that is frequently tangent to the earth at 18._____

    A. zero degrees longitude
    B. 90 degrees longitude
    C. 90 degrees latitude
    D. the equator

19. The Transverse Mercator Projection is used for the state plane coordinate system for states 19._____

    A. having conical shapes
    B. that are nearly square shaped
    C. that have greater north-south than east-west extent
    D. that have greater east-west than north-south extent

20. A vertical aerial photograph usually cannot be used as a map primarily because of 20._____

    A. blurred image and terrain relief
    B. improper focal length and improper height
    C. blurred image and incorrect height
    D. terrain relief and image tilt

21. Of the following statements relating to aerial photographs, the CORRECT answer is the 21._____

    A. smaller the scale, the smaller the area covered
    B. higher the altitude of the plane, the larger the scale of the photograph
    C. area covered by a fixed size photograph varies inversely as the square of the scale
    D. focal length of the camera is not a determining factor in the scale of the photograph

22. Rectification of an aerial photograph 22._____

    A. corrects for the ground not being flat
    B. eliminates error due to the airplane not being at the correct height when the photograph is taken
    C. corrects for error in the overlap of the photographs
    D. corrects for error due to the axis of the camera not being vertical when the shot was taken

23. An aerial photograph with distortions removed is termed a(n) 23._____

    A. isophoto
    B. planophoto
    C. orthophoto
    D. rectophoto

24. Viewing an object with one eye closed and then the other eye closed reveals a displacement of the object.
    This is known as

    A. double vision
    B. apparent displacement
    C. visual distortion
    D. parallax

25. A panchromatic emulsion used in aerial photography is

    A. red and white only
    B. blue, red and white
    C. black and white
    D. black, red, blue and white

KEY (CORRECT ANSWERS)

1. D
2. C
3. B
4. C
5. D

6. C
7. B
8. C
9. C
10. B

11. A
12. D
13. C
14. B
15. C

16. D
17. D
18. D
19. C
20. D

21. C
22. D
23. C
24. D
25. C

TEST 2

DIRECTIONS: Each question or incomplete statement is followed by several suggested answers or completions. Select the one that BEST answers the question or completes the statement. *PRINT THE LETTER OF THE CORRECT ANSWER IN THE SPACE AT THE RIGHT.*

1. In the diagram shown at the right, h equals

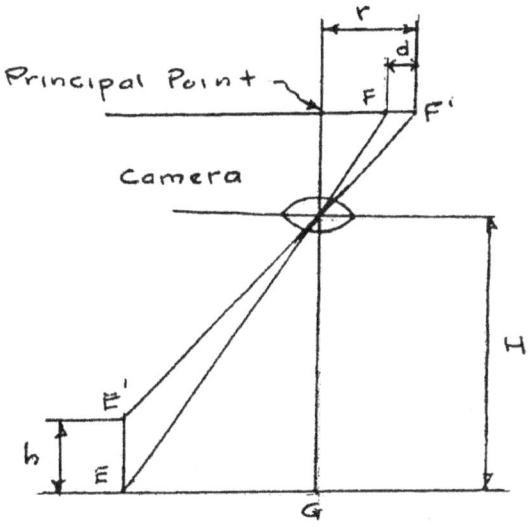

   A. dH/r
   B. rH/d
   C. dr/H
   D. H/dr

1.____

2. In the diagram for the previous problem, G is the

   A. nadir point B. low point
   C. zenith point D. ground zero

2.____

3. The focal length for a camera is 145 mm. Its focal length, in inches, is MOST NEARLY

   A. 5.65   B. 5.68   C. 5.71   D. 5.74

3.____

4. The MOST common size lens used in aerial photogrammetric mapping is

   A. 3.5"   B. 6"   C. 8.25"   D. 12"

4.____

5. A satellite used in acquiring land imagery from space is

   A. Telstar   B. Spot   C. Minos   D. Tiros

5.____

6. The sensors used on a satellite are usually

   A. mechanical-optical   B. electro-mechanical
   C. film based   D. electro-optical

6.____

7. A single detector on a satellite imager is a

   A. spacial resolution   B. spot
   C. photomultiplier   D. pixel

7.____

21

8. The scanner on a satellite imager scans

   A. across track
   B. parallel to the track
   C. first across track and then parallel to track
   D. first parallel to track and then across track

9. The Landsats 4 and 5 MSS have _____ bands.

   A. 5   B. 6   C. 7   D. 8

10. MSS is an abbreviation for

    A. multispectral scanner
    B. multisized spacers
    C. mechanical spectral scanner
    D. multispectral system

11. CCD is the abbreviation for

    A. charge-coupled devices
    B. charged capacitance detectors
    C. close-range couple detectors
    D. close-range charged devices

12. Of the following, the one that is a scanning mode is _____ sensors.

    A. linear array   B. image swath
    C. push-broom linear   D. close-range linear

13. A vertical aerial photograph was taken from a plane flying at an altitude of 5000 meters. The ground elevation is 276 meters. The focal length is 152.4 mm. The scale of the photograph is MOST NEARLY

    A. 1/31000   B. 1/32000   C. 1/33000   D. 1/34000

14. The effect of relief on the location of image points is known as

    A. relief tilt   B. relief effect
    C. parallax   D. relief displacement

15. The area in square inches of a 20 centimeters by 20 centimeters square is MOST NEARLY

    A. 62   B. 64   C. 66   D. 68

16. Some mosaics made from aerial photographs are quite inexact in scale, especially when

    A. there are grade crossing overpasses on the map
    B. there is considerable change in elevation on the ground
    C. a tall building appears on the mosaic
    D. the elevation of the plane changes while the photographs are taken

17. In aerial photography there is a film shift in the direction of flight during exposure whose purpose is to

    A. correct for timing inconsistency
    B. compensate for tilt
    C. minimize image blur
    D. compensate for drift

18. The intervalometer is set to insure the

    A. correct v/H
    B. correct amount of light enters the camera
    C. proper size of photographs
    D. proper overlap of adjacent photographs

19. CAD is an abbreviation for

    A. computer analog drafting
    B. calculation assisted drafting
    C. computer-aided design
    D. calculation assisted design

20. The analysis of aerial photographs and images for the purpose of extracting the best interpretation of the image content is the definition of

    A. quantitative photographic interpretation
    B. high resolution photography
    C. remote sensing
    D. image reflection

21. The number of degrees longitude the sun moves in one hour is

    A. 5   B. 10   C. 15   D. 20

22. The ecliptic is the projection on the surface of the earth of

    A. an asteroid   B. the North Star
    C. the moon   D. the sun

23. The plane of the earth's orbit around the sun is termed the orbit plane. The number of degrees that an axis perpendicular to the orbit plane goes through the center of the earth with the axis of the earth is MOST NEARLY

    A. 21 1/2   B. 23 1/2   C. 25 1/2   D. 27 1/2

24. Looking from above, the direction the sun moves about the earth in a year and the rotation of the earth about its axis is in a

    A. counterclockwise direction and the earth rotates about its axis in a counterclockwise direction
    B. counterclockwise direction and the earth rotates about its axis in a clockwise direction
    C. clockwise direction and the earth rotates about its axis in a counterclockwise direction
    D. clockwise direction and the earth rotates about its axis in a clockwise direction

25. A solstice can occur on

    A. March 21
    B. December 22
    C. January 1
    D. June 21

KEY (CORRECT ANSWERS)

1. A
2. A
3. C
4. B
5. B
6. D
7. D
8. A
9. C
10. A
11. A
12. C
13. A
14. D
15. A
16. B
17. C
18. D
19. C
20. C
21. C
22. D
23. B
24. C
25. D

TEST 3

DIRECTIONS: Each question or incomplete statement is followed by several suggested answers or completions. Select the one that BEST answers the question or completes the statement. *PRINT THE LETTER OF THE CORRECT ANSWER IN THE SPACE AT THE RIGHT.*

1. Metrology is the study of

    A. the earth's composition
    B. the earth's surface
    C. comets and meteors
    D. weights and measures

    1._____

2. The intersection of a tilted aerial photograph and a vertical photograph is an

    A. axis of inclination
    B. isocline
    C. isoline
    D. isocenter

    2._____

3. In a vertical aerial photograph with varying relief, the higher the relief the

    A. higher the scale and the higher the displacement
    B. higher the scale and the lower the displacement
    C. lower the relief and the higher the displacement
    D. lower the relief and the lower the displacement

    3._____

4. An instrument used to produce a photograph in which the tilt has been eliminated is a(n)

    A. orthophotographer
    B. rectifier
    C. stereoplotter
    D. monocomparator

    4._____

5. The instrument composed of a two-axis stage with a measuring microscope and coordinate readout is a

    A. stereoplotter
    B. monocomparator
    C. analytic plotter
    D. rectifier

    5._____

6. Softcopy as a restitution system is

    A. optical
    B. mechanical
    C. digital
    D. analytical

    6._____

7. 20°-18'-30" is, in decimals of a degree, MOST NEARLY

    A. 20.2783   B. 20.2883   C. 20.2983   D. 20.3083

    7._____

8. 21.5384° is, in degrees, minutes and seconds, MOST NEARLY

    A. 21°-32'-18.24"
    B. 21°-32'-5.12"
    C. 21°-31'-52.16"
    D. 21°-31'-23.18"

    8._____

9. The angle between the true meridian and the magnetic meridian is the magnetic

    A. dip
    B. declination
    C. inclination
    D. offset

    9._____

25

10. The method surveyors usually use in determining elevations on a construction job is _____ levelling.

   A. differential
   B. stadia
   C. reciprocal
   D. trigonometric

11. One radian is, in degrees, MOST NEARLY

   A. 57.2758   B. 57.2958   C. 57.3158   D. 57.3358

12. A planimeter is used to measure

   A. dip   B. strike   C. area   D. volume

13. Assume a circle has 400 degrees instead of the usual 360 degrees. Seventy-five degrees would be, on a 400 degree circle, MOST NEARLY in degrees

   A. 83.167   B. 83.25   C. 83.283   D. 83.333

14. The unit measurement of area in the metric system is the

   A. tesla   B. pascal   C. hectare   D. farad

15. One meter is, in inches, MOST NEARLY

   A. 39.37   B. 39.27   C. 39.17   D. 39.07

16. One inch, in centimeters, is

   A. 2.44   B. 2.54   C. 2.64   D. 2.34

17. A nautical mile is, in feet,

   A. 5966   B. 6000   C. 6046   D. 6076

18. One kilometer, in miles, is

   A. .57   B. .62   C. .67   D. .72

19. A chain is equal to_____ feet.

   A. 66   B. 68   C. 70   D. 72

20. The number of square feet in an acre is

   A. 43470   B. 43560   C. 43650   D. 43740

21. The number that must be added to $x^2 + 8x$ to complete the square is

   A. 16   B. 32   C. 48   D. 64

22. The area of an equilateral whose side is 9 is

   A. $\frac{49}{4}\sqrt{3}$ B. $\frac{16\sqrt{3}}{3}$ C. $\frac{81\sqrt{3}}{4}$ D. $27\sqrt{3}$

23. In the United States, the length or width of a normal township is _____ miles.

   A. 5   B. 6   C. 7   D. 8

24. A row of townships extending north and south is called a   24._____
    A. guide   B. vertical   C. tier   D. range

25. The area of a township, in square miles, is   25._____
    A. 25   B. 36   C. 49   D. 64

KEY (CORRECT ANSWERS)

1.	D	11.	B
2.	C	12.	C
3.	A	13.	D
4.	B	14.	C
5.	B	15.	A
6.	C	16.	B
7.	D	17.	D
8.	A	18.	B
9.	B	19.	A
10.	A	20.	B

21. A
22. C
23. B
24. D
25. B

TEST 4

DIRECTIONS: Each question or incomplete statement is followed by several suggested answers or completions. Select the one that BEST answers the question or completes the statement. *PRINT THE LETTER OF THE CORRECT ANSWER IN THE SPACE AT THE RIGHT.*

1. The right of the people or government to take private property for public use upon payment of just compensation is the definition of

   A. easement
   B. eminent domain
   C. encroachment
   D. escheat

2. An absolute or ownership in property including unlimited power of alienation is the definition of

   A. fee simple
   B. guarantee title
   C. general warrantee deed
   D. escheat

3. Within a deed is a designation of natural objects, monuments, course, distance or other matters of description as limits of the boundaries is the definition of

   A. appurtenances
   B. abstract of title
   C. metes and bounds description
   D. call

Questions 4-5.

DIRECTIONS: Questions 4 and 5 refer to the statement below.

"If you wish to sail from one port to another," a map maker wrote in the sixteenth century, "here is a chart, and a straight line on it, and if you follow this line carefully you will certainly arrive at your destination. But the length of the line may not be correct."

4. This line is called a(n) _____ line.

   A. azimuth
   B. true
   C. rhumb
   D. great circle

5. The projection used is usually a(n) _____ projection.

   A. albers
   B. conic
   C. Mercator
   D. Lambert

6. Topographic maps in the United States are made according to the _____ projection.

   A. Mercator
   B. polyconic
   C. cylindrical central
   D. cylindrical equal spaced

7. On a map the bearing of line EF is N18° E and the bearing of line EG is S67° W. Angle FEG is equal to, in degrees,

   A. 131
   B. 175
   C. 85
   D. 229

8. The radius of a circle in which a central angle of one degree subtends an arc of 100 feet is MOST NEARLY _____ feet.

   A. 5700   B. 5730   C. 5760   D. 5790

9. A magnetic azimuth of 54°-00' was observed along line EF in January 2000. The declination for the area is found from an isogonic chart dated 1990 to be 15°-30'E with an annual change of 2' westward. The true azimuth of line EF is

   A. 39°-10'E   B. 39°-30'E   C. 69°-10'E   D. 69°-50'E

10. If the scale on a map is 1:50000, a mile would be _____ inches.

    A. 1.21   B. 1.23   C. 1.25   D. 1.27

11. On a map there may be three norths: true north, magnetic north and _____ north.

    A. geodetic   B. geographic
    C. grid   D. mercator

12. In taping with a 100 foot steel tape, one end of the tape is one foot higher than the other end of the tape. This will introduce an error in measuring, in inches, MOST NEARLY

    A. 1/64   B. 1/32   C. 1/16   D. 1/8

13. $\sin(x+90°)$ is equal to

    A. $\sin x$ B. $\cos x$ C. $-\sin x$ D. $-\cos x$

14. $\cos^2 x - \sin^2 x$ is equal to

    A. $\sin 2x$ B. $-\sin 2x$ C. $\cos 2x$ D. $-\cos 2x$

15. The quadrant in which sin x and cos x are negative is

    A. I   B. II   C. III   D. IV

16. EDM is an abbreviation for electronic _____ measurement.

    A. direct   B. decimal   C. distance   D. data

17. In surveying with a level, a point used in the leveling process to temporarily transfer the elevation from one setup to the next is a

    A. PI   B. TP   C. FS   D. ES

18. Positional and navigational data from the GPS are provided to the community through PPS or SPS.
    SPS is the abbreviation for

    A. Selective Positioning System
    B. Stationary Positioning System
    C. Standard Positioning Service
    D. Standard Positioning System

19. The pattern of illuminated horizontal scanning lines formed on a television picture tube when no signal is being received is

   A. static   B. parallax   C. raster   D. overlap

19._____

20. Project planning starts with the maps to be produced. The restraints on the choices available to the planner are

   A. area to be covered and the cost of the end product
   B. accuracy of the maps and the cost of the maps
   C. use of airplanes or satellites and the precision of the maps
   D. the detailed information the map is to supply and the area to be covered

20._____

21. The technical name for the North Star is

   A. Arcturus   B. Andromeda
   C. Polaris   D. Vega

21._____

22. The constellation in which the North Star appears is

   A. Virgo   B. Cassiopeia
   C. Ursa Major D. Ursa Minor

22._____

23. A right cone is cut by a plane perpendicular to the base of the cone. The curve formed by the intersection of the surface of the cone and the plane is a

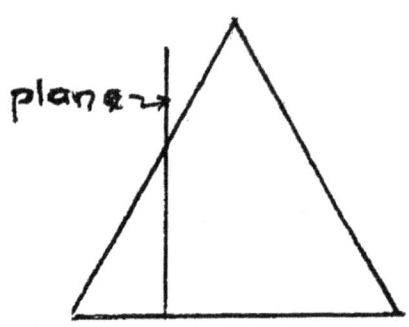

   A. hyperbola
   B. parabola
   C. half of an ellipse
   D. none of the above

23._____

24. A topographic map has a scale of one inch equals 40 feet. The contours are every 5 feet. The horizontal distance between two adjacent contours is 3/4 inch. The slope of the earth at that line is, in degrees, MOST NEARLY

   A. 9 1/2   B. 11 1/2   C. 13 1/2   D. 15 1/2

24._____

25. $\sin \frac{x}{2}$ is equal to

   A. $\dfrac{\sqrt{1+\cos x}}{2}$ B. $\dfrac{\sqrt{1-\cos x}}{2}$ C. $\sqrt{\dfrac{1+\cos x}{2}}$ D. $\sqrt{\dfrac{1-\cos x}{2}}$

25._____

KEY (CORRECT ANSWERS)

1.	B	11.	C
2.	A	12.	C
3.	D	13.	B
4.	C	14.	C
5.	C	15.	C
6.	B	16.	C
7.	A	17.	B
8.	B	18.	C
9.	C	19.	C
10.	D	20.	B

21. C
22. D
23. A
24. A
25. B

EXAMINATION SECTION
TEST 1

DIRECTIONS: Each question or incomplete statement is followed by several suggested answers or completions. Select the one that BEST answers the question or completes the statement. *PRINT THE LETTER OF THE CORRECT ANSWER IN THE SPACE AT THE RIGHT.*

1. If a map has a scale of 1" = 1 mile, a fractional equivalent would be

   A. $\dfrac{1}{63360}$ B. $\dfrac{1}{5280}$ C. $\dfrac{1}{1000}$ D. $\dfrac{1}{1200}$

2. The diameter of the earth is MOST NEARLY _____ miles.

   A. 5,000 B. 6,000 C. 7,000 D. 8,000

3. An instrument used to reproduce a drawing at a different scale is called a

   A. psychrometer B. manometer
   C. planimeter D. pantograph

4. A baseline is measured many times and the length was found to be 594.32 ± .01'. This reading means

   A. none of the measurements was less than 594.31' nor more than 594.33'
   B. 594.32' is not the accepted measurement of the length
   C. ±.01 is a measure of the accuracy of 594.32'
   D. 594.32' is two standard deviations from 594.32'

5. The engineering societies have accepted the metric system for use in engineering design. This was done despite the fact that

   A. the metric system is easy to use
   B. it will be easy to switch from the current system
   C. it is easy for tradesmen to build based on metric measurements
   D. the United States remains one of the few countries not using the metric system

6. One radian is MOST NEARLY _____ degrees.

   A. 56.3 B. 57.3 C. 58.3 D. 59.3

7. Of the following statements relating to the hkrdhess of pencil leads, the one that is CORRECT is

   A. B is harder than H B. HB is harder than H
   C. F is harder than HB D. B is harder than HB

8. A 24" x 36" drafting paper has a 1/2 inch boundary. To check that the rectangle is not skewed, the BEST method is to

   A. check that the rectangle is exactly 1/2 inch from the edge of the paper
   B. check that the diagonals of the rectangle are equal in measure
   C. measure the opposite sides of the rectangle to insure they are equal
   D. use a T-square and triangles to insure the opposite sides are parallel

9. Using a 30°-60°-90° right triangle and a 45 right triangle, it is relatively easy to draw an angle of _____ degrees.   9.____

   A. 15   B. 25   C. 35   D. 55

10. The angle that the needle on the compass of a transit makes with the true meridian is termed the _____ of the needle.   10.____

   A. inclination   B. variation
   C. offset   D. declination

11. The _____ line contains the points of zero magnetic deviation from true North.   11.____

   A. zero dip   B. secular variation
   C. true magnetic bearing D. agonic

12. The contour map of a hill is shown at the right. The shape of the hill is MOST NEARLY a(n)   12.____

   A. cone
   B. hemisphere
   C. paraboloid
   D. ellipsoid

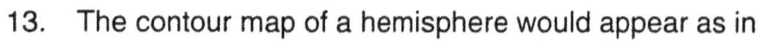

13. The contour map of a hemisphere would appear as in   13.____

A.

B.

C.

D.

14.

Contour Crossing
A Street

Of the following, the contour that is CORRECT is

A.   B.

C.   D.

15. *An outstanding claim or encumbrance which if valid will affect or impair the owner's title* defines

    A. condemnation
    B. demise
    C. consequential damage
    D. cloud of title

16. *The body of principles developed from immemorial usage and custom which receive judicial recognition and sanction through repeated application* is the definition of _____ law.

    A. legislated
    B. de facto
    C. common
    D. historic

17. *An absolute estate or ownership in property including unlimited power of alienation* is the definition of

    A. guarantee title
    B. fee simple
    C. general warranty deed
    D. grantee

18. ———x———x———x on a map represents a(n)

    A. discontinued road
    B. overhead power line
    C. hedge
    D. fence

19. —+—+—+—+—+— on a map represents a

    A. discontinued road
    B. property line that was eliminated
    C. railroad
    D. power line

20. One acre is equal to _____ square feet.

    A. 42,650   B. 42,560   C. 43,650   D. 43,560

21. Liber is a

    A. map   B. deed   C. plan   D. book

22. Riparian rights are rights to

    A. minerals under the land
    B. sinking wells to draw water from the aquafer
    C. gain access to their property
    D. of waterfront land in the use of the bed and banks of the water

23. A rod is equal to _____ yards.

    A. 4 1/2   B. 5   C. 5 1/2   D. 6

24. A planimeter is used to measure

    A. area   B. angles
    C. bearings   D. the length of lines

25. A chain is a unit of land measurement equal to _____ feet.

    A. 60   B. 62   C. 64   D. 66

KEY (CORRECT ANSWERS)

1. A	11. D
2. D	12. A
3. D	13. B
4. C	14. D
5. D	15. D
6. B	16. C
7. C	17. B
8. B	18. D
9. A	19. C
10. D	20. D

21. D
22. D
23. C
24. A
25. D

TEST 2

DIRECTIONS: Each question or incomplete statement is followed by several suggested answers or completions. Select the one that BEST answers the question or completes the statement. *PRINT THE LETTER OF THE CORRECT ANSWER IN THE SPACE AT THE RIGHT.*

1. Eminent domain is defined as

   A. the government's position prevailing in a dispute with an individual
   B. the original ownership of property in the government
   C. an instrument in writing by which property is transferred from a private party to the government
   D. the right of government to take private property for public use upon payment of just compensation

    1.____

2. 32°-20"-30" is equal to

   A. 32.3417   B. 32.3503   C. 32.3587   D. 32.3617

    2.____

3. 34.5120 degrees is equal to

   A. 34°-30'-43.2"   B. 34°-30'-53.2"
   C. 34°-31'-03.2"   D. 34°-31'-13.2"

    3.____

4. .01 feet is MOST NEARLY _____ inch(es).

   A. 1/8   B. 5/32   C. 3/16   D. 7/32

    4.____

5. One inch is equal to _____ centimeters.

   A. 2.44   B. 2.54   C. 2.64   D. 2.74

    5.____

Questions 6-8

DIRECTIONS: Questions 6 to 8, inclusive, refer to the field notes for a quadrilateral ABCD.

Line	Length	Bearing
AB	50.00	N30°-00'E
BC	80.00	S60°-00'E
CD	130.00	S30°-00'N
DA		

6. The area of the quadrilateral is equal to _____ square feet.

   A. 7,000   B. 7,200   C. 7,400   D. 7,600

    6.____

7. The bearing of line DA is

   A. N10°-00'W   B. N15°-00'W   C. N20°-00'W   D. N30°-00'W

    7.____

8. The length of DA is _____ feet.

   A. 113.14   B. 115.14   C. 117.14   D. 119.14

    8.____

2 (#2)

9. Of the following, the instrument MOST closely related to a transit is a

   A. level
   B. plane table
   C. sextant
   D. theodolite

10. Azimuth is usually measured _____ from the _____.

    A. clockwise; south
    B. counterclockwise; south
    C. clockwise; north
    D. counterclockwise; north

11. The usual length of a steel surveying tape is _____ feet.

    A. 50
    B. 75
    C. 100
    D. 200

12. The number of yards in a mile is

    A. 1,740
    B. 1,750
    C. 1,760
    D. 1,770

13. The scale of a drawing is one inch equals one foot. The scale ratio of the drawing is

    A. 1/12
    B. 1/144
    C. 1/48
    D. 1/192

14. 0° longitude goes through the city of

    A. Greenwich, England
    B. London, England
    C. Paris, France
    D. Versailles, France

15. A _____ map shows the configuration of the terrain and location of natural and man-made objects.

    A. geographic
    B. hydrographic
    C. geodetic
    D. topographic

16. The geometric shape of the earth is MOST NEARLY a(n)

    A. part of a paraboloid
    B. sphere
    C. ellipsoid
    D. part of a hyperboloid

17. New York City is at latitude

    A. 35° N
    B. 40° N
    C. 45° N
    D. 50° N

18. New York City is at longitude

    A. 62° W
    B. 66° W
    C. 70° W
    D. 74° W

19. The Mercator projection is frequently used for maps in high school textbooks. The disadvantage in using Mercator projection is that

    A. directions are distorted
    B. the greatest distortion is at the equator
    C. longitudes are inaccurate
    D. areas are distorted

20. The MOST commonly used projection in the world for engineering work is the _____ projection.

    A. Mercator
    B. Albers conformal
    C. Lambert conformal conic
    D. Thales

Questions 21-25.

DIRECTIONS: Questions 21 through 25, inclusive, refer to the diagram below.

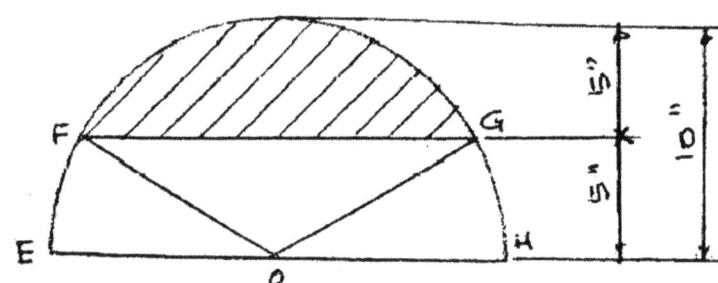

21. The area of the semicircle is MOST NEARLY _____ square inches.   21._____
    A. 151   B. 153   C. 155   D. 157

22. The area of triangle FOG is MOST NEARLY _____ square inches.   22._____
    A. 41.3   B. 43.3   C. 45.3   D. 47.3

23. Angle EOF is _____ degrees.   23._____
    A. 20   B. 25   C. 30   D. 35

24. The area of the sector EOF is _____ square inches.   24._____
    A. 26.2   B. 28.2   C. 30.2   D. 32.2

25. The shaded area is, in square inches, MOST NEARLY   25._____
    A. 55.3   B. 57.3   C. 49.3   D. 61.3

KEY (CORRECT ANSWERS)

1.	D	11.	C
2.	A	12.	C
3.	A	13.	A
4.	A	14.	A
5.	B	15.	D
6.	B	16.	C
7.	B	17.	B
8.	A	18.	D
9.	D	19.	D
10.	C	20.	C
21.	D		
22.	B		
23.	C		
24.	A		
25.	D		

EXAMINATION SECTION
TEST 1

DIRECTIONS: Each question or incomplete statement is followed by several suggested answers or completions. Select the one that BEST answers the question or completes the statement. *PRINT THE LETTER OF THE CORRECT ANSWER IN THE SPACE AT THE RIGHT.*

Questions 1-5.

DIRECTIONS: Questions 1 through 5 are based on the table shown below.

POPULATION, URBAN AND RURAL, BY RACE: 2000 TO 2020

In thousands, except percent. An urbanized area comprises at least 1 city of 50,000 inhabitants (central city) plus contiguous, closely settled areas (urban fringe). Data for 2000 and 2010 according to urban definition used in the 2010 census; 2020 data according to the 2020 definition.

YEAR AND AREA	TOTAL	WHITE	ALL OTHER	PERCENT DISTRIBUTION TOTAL	WHITE	ALL OTHER
2000, total population	151,326	135,150	16,176	100.0	100.0	100.0
Urban	96,847	86,864	9,983	64.0	64.3	61.7
Inside urbanized areas	69,249	61,925	7,324	45.8	45.8	45.3
Central cities	48,377	42,042	6,335	32.0	31.1	39.2
Urban fringe	20,872	19,883	989	13.8	14.7	6.1
Outside urbanized areas	27,598	24,939	2,659	18.2	18.5	16.4
Rural	54,479	48,286	6,193	36.0	35.7	38.3
2010, total population	179,323	158,832	20,491	100.0	100.0	100.0
Urban	125,269	110,428	14,840	69.9	69.5	72.4
Inside urbanized areas	95,848	83,770	12,079	53.5	52.7	58.9
Central cities	57,975	47,627	10,348	32.3	30.0	50.5
Urban fringe	37,873	36,143	1,371	21.1	22.8	8.4
Outside urbanized areas	29,420	26,658	2,762	16.4	16.8	13.5
Rural	54,054	48,403	5,651	30.1	30.5	27.6
2020, total population	203,212	177,749	25,463	100.0	100.0	100.0
Urban	149,325	128,773	20,552	73.5	72.4	80.7
Inside urbanized areas	118,447	100,952	17,495	58.3	56.8	68.7
Central cities	63,922	49,547	14,375	31.5	27.9	56.5
Urban fringe	54,525	51,405	3,120	26.8	28.9	12.3
Outside urbanized areas	30,878	27,822	3,057	15.2	15.7	12.0
Rural	53,887	48,976	4,911	26.5	27.6	19.3

1. The ratio of urban to rural population in 2000 was MOST NEARLY   1._____

    A. 3:1   B. 4:1   C. 2:1   D. 14:1

2. According to the table, the trend of population inside urban areas has been   2._____

    A. towards greater concentration   B. towards less concentration
    C. towards stabilization   D. erratic

3. Since 2000, the urban fringe white population has substantially increased while the urban fringe other population has

   A. slightly decreased
   B. greatly decreased
   C. remained the same
   D. increased moderately

4. Over the years, the percentage of the urban white population as compared with the percentage of the total urban population has

   A. remained relatively constant
   B. substantially decreased
   C. substantially increased
   D. varied

5. Select the one of the following which BEST describes the central city white population rate of decrease since 2000 as compared with the central city black population rate of increase.

   A. The central city white population rate of decrease has been greater than the central city black population rate of increase.
   B. The central city white and black populations have not increased to a significant degree.
   C. The central city white population rate of decrease has been equal to the central city black population rate of increase.
   D. The central city white population rate of decrease has been less than the central city black population rate of increase.

Questions 6-10.

DIRECTIONS: Questions 6 through 10 are to be answered on the basis of the table shown below.

STANDARDS FOR RECREATION AREAS

TYPE OF AREA	ACRES PER 1,000 POPULATION	SIZE OF SITE (ACRES) IDEAL	SIZE OF SITE (ACRES) MINIMUM	RADIUS OF AREA SERVED (MILES)
Playgrounds	1.5	4	2	0.5
Neighborhood parks	2.0	10	5	0.5
Playfields	1.5	15	10	1.5
Community parks	3.5	100	40	2.0
District parks	2.0	200	100	3.0
Regional parks and reservations	15.0	500-1,000	varies	10.0

6. What is the MINIMUM number of playfields that a community of 15,000 people may contain if the size of each is kept within the limits shown in the table?

   A. 4   B. 10   C. 6   D. 2

7. If, as far as possible, ideal sized playgrounds are built, how many IDEAL SIZED playgrounds should a community of 12,000 people contain?

   A. 4   B. 8   C. 1   D. 10

8. Approximately how many people can a community park of 200 acres serve? 8.____

   A. 120,000   B. 80,000   C. 55,000   D. 20,000

9. If only minimum sized neighborhood parks are built, how many will be required for a population of 20,000? 9.____

   A. 5   B. 2   C. 8   D. 12

10. A community of 75,000 persons is evenly distributed over a 5 square mile area. Of the following, the number and size of playgrounds that would BEST satisfy the standards is _____ playgrounds @ _____ acres each. 10.____

    A. 5; 7.5   B. 35; 3.5   C. 10; 10   D. 50; 1.5

11. The illustration shown at the right is an example of a 11.____

    A. simple grade separation
    B. simple interchange of a freeway with a highway
    C. three-level interchange
    D. T interchange

12. The practical MINIMUM number of cars per hour that can be carried per lane on a limited access roadway with uninterrupted flow is considered to be APPROXIMATELY 12.____

    A. 750   B. 1,500   C. 5,000   D. 10,000

13. A street that is open at only one end, with provision for a turn-around at the other, is called a 13.____

    A. local street   B. cul-de-sac
    C. loop street   D. minor street

14. Which of the following shopping center types is the local source of staple goods and daily services? 14.____

    A. Central Business District
    B. Regional Shopping Center
    C. Highway Strip Development
    D. Neighborhood Shopping Center

15. *Air rights* refers to the concept that 15.____

    A. all people are entitled to clean air
    B. vistas from apartments cannot be obstructed
    C. buildings can be constructed over railroads or highways
    D. buildings should be oriented towards the prevailing breezes

16. The one of the following LEAST likely to be considered an integral part of urban design is 16.____

    A. spatial forms   B. surfaces
    C. vistas   D. underground utilities

Questions 17-21.

DIRECTIONS: Questions 17 through 21 are based upon the table shown below.

LIVE BIRTHS, DEATHS, MARRIAGES, AND DIVORCES: 1940-1991

	Number (1,000)					Rate per 1,000 Population				
		DEATHS		MAR-	DIVOR-		DEATHS		MAR-	DIVOR-
YEAR	BIRTHS	TOTAL	INFANT	RIAGES	CES	BIRTHS	TOTAL	INFANT	RIAGES	CES
1940	2,777	697	(NA)	948	83	30.1	14.7	(NA)	10.3	0.9
1945	2,965	816	78	1,008	104	29.5	13.2	99.9	10.0	1.0
1950	2,950	1,118	130	1,274	171	27.7	13.0	85.8	12.0	1.6
1955	2,909	1,192	135	1,188	175	25.1	11.7	71.7	10.3	1.5
1960	2,618	1,327	142	1,127	196	21.3	11.3	64.6	9.2	1.6
1965	2,377	1,393	120	1,327	218	18.7	10.9	55.7	10.4	1.7
1970	2,559	1,417	111	1,596	264	19.4	10.8	47.0	12.1	2.0
1975	2,858	1,402	105	1,613	485	20.4	10.6	38.3	12.2	3.5
1980	3,632	1,452	104	1,667	385	24.1	9.6	29.2	11.1	2.6
1985	4,104	1,529	107	1,531	377	25.0	9.3	26.4	9.3	2.3
1990	4,258	1,712	111	1,523	393	23.7	9.5	26.0	8.5	2.2
1991	4,268	1,702	108	1,548	414	23.3	9.3	25.3	8.5	2.3

NA   Not Available

17. From 1940 to 1991, the birth rate has

    A. approximately doubled
    B. remained stable
    C. been reduced by 25%
    D. had two breaks in its downward progression

18. A comparison of the total population death rate to the infant death rate shows that

    A. the two rates have remained constant
    B. the infant death rate is greater
    C. the total population death rate has decreased at a faster rate
    D. infants had a greater chance to survive in 1965 than in 1980

19. In 1945, about one marriage out of 10 ended in divorce.
    In which of the following years would the rate be LESS?

    A. 1985   B. 1965   C. 1950   D. 1940

20. The significance of the decrease in the infant death rate is that

    A. family size will increase
    B. family size will decrease
    C. family size will not be affected
    D. children will become a smaller percentage of the total population

21. According to the chart, the total death rate declined from 14.7 in 1940 to 9.3 in 1991, yet each year more people have died. This fact is MOST likely accounted for by

    A. poor reporting techniques
    B. the decrease in the mortality rate
    C. the increase of total population
    D. the increase of older people in the total population

22. The type of interchange pictured in the illustration shown at the right is called a _____ interchange.

    A. simple
    B. cloverleaf
    C. universal
    D. Bel Geddes

22._____

23. This type of interchange (pictured in the preceding question) is used when

    A. topographic conditions are difficult
    B. traffic volumes are heavy
    C. a major and minor road intersect
    D. two major roads intersect

23._____

24. The one of the following basic requirements which would NOT be considered an integral part of a comprehensive plan is

    A. a capital improvement program
    B. physical design proposals
    C. long-range policy statements
    D. social and economic considerations

24._____

Questions 25-28.

DIRECTIONS: Questions 25 through 28 are based on the data shown below, which indicates total housing units.

HOUSING UNITS: 1960 to 1990
NUMBER IN THOUSANDS

▯▯▯ TOTAL   ≡ INSIDE SMSA'S   ▭ IN CENTRAL CITIES

(SMSA's = Standard Metropolitan Statistical Areas)

1990
- Total: 68,679
- Inside SMSA's: 46,295
- In Central Cities: 22,594

1980
- Total: 58,326
- Inside SMSA's: 36,386
- In Central Cities: 19,622

1970
- Total: 45,983
- Inside SMSA's: 25,626
- In Central Cities: 15,120

1960
- Total: 37,326

25. The period of GREATEST production of housing units was

  A. 1950-60   B. 1980-90   C. 1970-80   D. 1960-70

26. The location of the LARGEST gains in housing units since 1960 was in the

  A. suburban areas   B. central cities
  C. SMSA's   D. rural areas

27. Contrary to many misconceptions, the above data shows that the central cities are

  A. losing population to the suburbs
  B. keeping pace with the overall housing development
  C. showing strong development trends
  D. growing, but at a decreasing rate

28. Based on the above data, which of the following statements is MOST accurate? 28.____

    A. The housing stock is rapidly becoming outdated.
    B. More new homes are located in suburban areas than in central cities.
    C. The housing supply is rapidly catching up to the demand.
    D. The majority of the population is located in the SMSA's.

29. The name of the long-range schedule of major projects and their estimated costs over a period of 5-10 years is the 29.____

    A. budget
    B. comprehensive plan
    C. capital improvement program
    D. input-output program

30. *Cost Benefit Analysis* is a method used to 30.____

    A. determine budget compliance
    B. compare costs and benefits of a particular investment
    C. evaluate productivity in school construction
    D. establish social benefits for a neighborhood

31. A *workable program* is a SIGNIFICANT element of a(n) 31.____

    A. urban renewal program
    B. comprehensive plan
    C. capital improvement program
    D. urban design program

32. Which of the following would NOT be considered a major type of municipal planning agency in the United States? 32.____

    A. An independent planning commission
    B. The planning department
    C. A community development department
    D. A local renewal agency

33. Townhouses are MOST closely related to which of the following types of residential construction? 33.____

    A. Garden apartments   B. Row houses
    C. High-rise complexes   D. Semi-attached houses

34. The one of the following which could NOT be considered an accessory use in a residence district is a 34.____

    A. garage   B. greenhouse
    C. dwelling   D. storage shed

35. The ratio of parking space to retail floor area in a major regional shopping center would MOST often be 35.____

    A. 1:1   B. 3:1   C. 6:1   D. 10:1

KEY (CORRECT ANSWERS)

1. C
2. A
3. D
4. A
5. D

6. D
7. A
8. C
9. C
10. B

11. A
12. B
13. B
14. D
15. C

16. D
17. C
18. B
19. D
20. C

21. C
22. B
23. D
24. A
25. C

26. A
27. D
28. B
29. C
30. B

31. A
32. D
33. B
34. C
35. B

# TEST 2

DIRECTIONS: Each question or incomplete statement is followed by several suggested answers or completions. Select the one that BEST answers the question or completes the statement. *PRINT THE LETTER OF THE CORRECT ANSWER IN THE SPACE AT THE RIGHT.*

1. When the term *density* is commonly employed as a measure of land use, it refers to the   1.____

   A. number of persons   B. land coverage
   C. number of buildings   D. number of dwelling units

2. The *City Beautiful* movement was an outgrowth of the   2.____

   A. Bauhaus School in 1920
   B. Chicago World's Fair in 1893
   C. N.Y.C. Zoning Ordinance of 1916
   D. planning concepts of Emilio Sitte

3. The American Greenbelt towns were built to   3.____

   A. create open space
   B. establish independent satellite communities
   C. establish residential *dormitory* communities
   D. disperse urban population

4. The FIRST United States Housing Act was passed by Congress in   4.____

   A. 1929   B. 1949   C. 1941   D. 1937

5. A specific ratio of permissible floor space to lot area is known as   5.____

   A. floor area ratio   B. open space ratio
   C. sky exposure plane   D. lot coverage

6. A *protective covenant* can BEST be described as a(n)   6.____

   A. zoning ordinance   B. easement
   C. fire insurance policy   D. deed restriction

7. Underground utility lines are PREFERRED by most planners rather than overhead lines because underground lines   7.____

   A. are more accessible for maintenance
   B. cost less
   C. are not visible
   D. are laid in proper easements

8. If a local street right-of-way is 50 feet, the paved width of the street is GENERALLY _____ feet.   8.____

   A. 18   B. 26   C. 44   D. 50

49

9. The term *zero population growth* refers to the concept that

    A. the population will eventually become extinct
    B. married couples will not bear children
    C. each family will produce only two children
    D. parents will be subject to a planned schedule of parenthood

10. The MOST common dimensions of a half-acre residential lot are

    A. 100 ft. x 100 ft. B. 100 ft. x 200 ft.
    C. 120 ft. x 150 ft. D. 200 ft. x 200 ft.

11. As a general rule, large street trees should be planted

    A. 25 feet apart B. 50-75 feet apart
    C. 150-200 feet apart D. spaced randomly

12. A key regulation of a zoning ordinance relates to the

    A. architectural style of a building
    B. slope of a site
    C. height and bulk of buildings
    D. subsoil conditions

13. Under which one of the following authorities are zoning ordinances adopted by local communities?

    A. Police power B. Community power
    C. Will of the people D. Common law

14. MOST state enabling laws require that zoning regulations be based upon a

    A. land use plan B. base map
    C. comprehensive plan D. topographical map

15. The OBJECTIVE of an *interim zoning ordinance* is to

    A. zone only a portion of the community for a special purpose
    B. maintain existing conditions until a more comprehensive ordinance is prepared
    C. create a special district
    D. allow greater freedom in interpretation and utilization of the zoning regulations

16. A *non-conforming* use is

    A. a use which requires special approval to remain
    B. a building that does not comply with yard or bulk regulations
    C. one that is not permitted in a specific district
    D. a building which is structurally unsafe

17. A variance is granted by a board of appeals to

    A. obtain financial relief
    B. provide a balance of power
    C. test community opinion
    D. relieve practical difficulty and hardship

3 (#2)

18. Which of the following zoning regulations, taken by itself, would permit the MOST floor area of building on a specific lot? 18.____
A

   A. floor area ratio of 3:1
   B. maximum lot coverage of 60%
   C. maximum building height of 50 feet
   D. parking ratio of 2:1

19. Sewers used to carry rain or surface water to a body of water so as to prevent flooding are called _____ sewers. 19.____

   A. sanitary   B. storm   C. combined   D. overflow

20. The *Garden City* concept was made famous through a book written by 20.____

   A. Sir Patrick Abercombie   B. Patrick Geddes
   C. Ebenezer Howard   D. Sir Raymond Unwin

21. *Broadacre City* was advocated as a concept of urban development by 21.____

   A. F.L. Wright   B. Corbusier
   C. Saarinen   D. Geddes

22. The man who can BEST be associated with the planning principle of *high density-low coverage* is 22.____

   A. Wright   B. VanderRohe
   C. Saarinen   D. Corbusier

23. The AVERAGE number of persons per household in the United States in 1970 was MOST NEARLY 23.____

   A. 2.0   B. 2.5   C. 3.0   D. 3.5

24. Which of the following methods would be the MOST accurate in making population projections? 24.____

   A. Migration and natural increase
   B. Apportionment
   C. School enrollment
   D. Geometric extrapolation

25. According to the 1990 census, the total population of the United States was MOST NEARLY _____ million persons. 25.____

   A. 190   B. 200   C. 280   D. 350

26. After the amounts of different land uses in a medium-size city have been tabulated, which of the following percentages of the total developed land would USUALLY be utilized for streets? 26.____

   A. 12%   B. 20%   C. 30%   D. 8%

27. During the past twenty years, the MOST significant factor causing reorientation of traditional urban land use patterns has been

    A. express highway construction
    B. airport development
    C. new schools
    D. permissive zoning ordinances

28. The fundamental objective of MOST suburban communities in attracting new industries is to

    A. increase local employment opportunities
    B. attract minority groups to relocate
    C. establish a balanced land use pattern
    D. increase tax income

29. Which of the following terms is NOT considered to be part of the street classification system?

    A. Major street
    B. Right-of-way
    C. Local street
    D. Cul-de-sac

30. The USUAL purpose for providing a water tower in a municipal water supply system is to

    A. establish a constant pressure
    B. increase the supply of water
    C. increase water pressure
    D. provide a reserve supply

31. The neighborhood unit concept, which includes the elementary school as its major element, was FIRST advocated in 1929 by

    A. Clarence Stein
    B. Henry Wright
    C. Clarence Perry
    D. N. Engelhardt

32. In the past few years, the type of housing which has received the LEAST amount of consideration in resolving the housing problem is

    A. cluster housing
    B. urban renewal
    C. public housing
    D. middle-income housing

33. *Performance standards* have become an INTEGRAL part of zoning ordinances relating to

    A. road construction
    B. industrial districts
    C. parking garages
    D. commercial areas

34. The legal concept upon which the exercise of *condemnation* is based is called the

    A. *due process* clause of the Constitution
    B. police power
    C. power of eminent domain
    D. general community welfare

35. In which of the following situations would the granting of a zoning variance be considered as IMPROPER action? A(n)

    A. serious topographic condition
    B. undersized lot held prior to zoning
    C. subsurface water condition
    D. economic loss due to a zone change

KEY (CORRECT ANSWERS)

1.	D	16.	C
2.	B	17.	D
3.	C	18.	B
4.	D	19.	B
5.	A	20.	C
6.	D	21.	A
7.	C	22.	D
8.	B	23.	B
9.	C	24.	A
10.	B	25.	C
11.	B	26.	C
12.	C	27.	A
13.	A	28.	D
14.	C	29.	B
15.	B	30.	A

31. C
32. C
33. B
34. C
35. D

TEST 3

DIRECTIONS: Each question or incomplete statement is followed by several suggested answers or completions. Select the one that BEST answers the question or completes the statement. *PRINT THE LETTER OF THE CORRECT ANSWER IN THE SPACE AT THE RIGHT.*

1. The MAJOR objective of cluster zoning is to provide

    A. greater densities
    B. a variety of housing types
    C. open space
    D. racial balance

    1.___

2. One tool in combating the problems of *spread city* is to provide

    A. improved mass transportation systems
    B. more major highways
    C. more single-family detached houses
    D. more community facilities

    2.___

3. The Environmental Protection Agency has issued national air quality standards for six common pollutants. The one of the following pollutants NOT included is

    A. sulfur oxides
    B. carbon monoxide
    C. sulfur dioxide
    D. hydrocarbon oxides

    3.___

4. The national air quality standards have been issued in two parts: primary and secondary standards. A PRIMARY standard is designed to

    A. protect public health
    B. protect public welfare
    C. establish ambient air quality
    D. prevent damage to the environment

    4.___

5. The MAJOR source of air pollution in many urban areas, according to the Environmental Protection Agency, is

    A. emissions from new plants
    B. fossil-fueled steam-generating plants
    C. motor vehicles
    D. large incinerators

    5.___

6. A technique designed for the analysis of national economies and which employs an industry interaction model appearing in the form of a multi-sector or industrial matrix is called

    A. economic base theory
    B. industrial complex analysis
    C. calculated forecasting
    D. input-output theory

    6.___

7. The traditional master plan, with its strong emphasis on physical improvements, is being more frequently replaced by

    A. policies planning
    B. normative planning
    C. quantitative analysis
    D. flexible planning

8. *Advocate planning* involves the planner in

    A. participating on a federal level to influence local officials
    B. working within the planning unit to obtain his desired goals
    C. working as a citizen, often as a protagonist against the local government
    D. preparing mathematical models of urban development

9. Of the following, the type of commercial development which is LEAST likely to be planned is a

    A. regional shopping center
    B. local shopping complex
    C. highway strip development
    D. central business district

10. The *official map* of a community designates all of the following EXCEPT

    A. street right-of-ways
    B. parks and playgrounds
    C. residential areas
    D. school sites

11. Land use intensity standards are MOST appropriately utilized with the development of

    A. standard subdivisions
    B. planned unit developments
    C. mobile home parks
    D. high-rise residential complexes

12. A topographic map does NOT generally express

    A. climatic conditions
    B. easements
    C. boundary lines and distances
    D. existing buildings

13. Clarence Stein contributed GREATLY to the development of

    A. the concept of the balanced community
    B. the design of Reston
    C. high-rise residential complexes
    D. the Radburn Plan

14. In site development, a 10% grade is considered MAXIMUM for

    A. streets and roads
    B. play fields
    C. building sites
    D. parking lots

15. The Model Cities Program includes all of the following EXCEPT

    A. job training in construction work
    B. local control of programs
    C. physical and social rehabilitation of a community
    D. new city design and development

16. HUD's *Operation Breakthrough* program encouraged

    A. fireproof buildings
    B. innovative prefabricated systems of construction
    C. speed of building erection
    D. a socio-economic assault on the housing program

17. A condominium can BEST be described as a

    A. high-rise residential complex with a complete range of amenities
    B. variation of cooperative ownership
    C. planned unit development with open space
    D. building with full ownership of the dwelling unit and common ownership of public areas

18. A MAJOR advantage of a leaching cesspool is that it

    A. can be used where ground water is two feet below grade
    B. can be used close to potable water
    C. requires a minimum of land area
    D. is limited in capacity

19. Land which rises 2 feet vertically to 5 feet horizontally has a slope of

    A. 2.5%   B. 20%   C. 25%   D. 40%

20. The MAJOR advantage of a subsoil disposal bed for sewage disposal is that it

    A. may be used in any soil except that rated as impervious
    B. is more economical to build
    C. requires less land area than that of a treatment plant
    D. may have a ground water level less than 2 feet below grade

21. To achieve the GREATEST amount of open space in the siting of houses, the one of the following patterns that a planner would MOST probably choose is a _____ pattern.

    A. gridiron   B. court
    C. cluster   D. free-form

22. The maximum distance a child should be required to walk to an elementary school is GENERALLY considered to be _____ mile.

    A. 1/4   B. 1/2   C. 3/4   D. 1

23. Modern industrial parks most often will include all of the following amenities EXCEPT   23.____

    A. landscaping and screening
    B. employee parking areas
    C. utilities and services
    D. multi-story structures

24. The BEST source of aerial photographs that provide the greatest coverage of the United   24.____
    States by a single agency is the

    A. Soil Conservation Service
    B. U.S. National Ocean Survey
    C. National Park Service
    D. Agricultural Stabilization Conservation Service

25. Terrain analysis is MOST closely related to the study of   25.____

    A. landforms   B. drainage
    C. soil   D. land erosion

26. Riparian rights deal with property that is located   26.____

    A. over mineral resources   B. along a body of water
    C. over railroad tracks   D. over a right-of-way

27. The ADVANTAGE of a *stol* port is that it   27.____

    A. can be located near another airport
    B. is not government regulated
    C. accommodates business and pleasure aircraft
    D. requires a short runway

28. One square mile contains EXACTLY _____ acres.   28.____

    A. 316   B. 444   C. 640   D. 1,000

29. The one of the following methods of refuse disposal that causes the LEAST air pollution,   29.____
    if efficiently carried out, is

    A. open dumping   B. land fill
    C. incineration   D. compositing

30. Sewers which collect sewage only from the plumbing systems of buildings and carry it to   30.____
    a sewage treatment plant are called _____ sewers.

    A. sanitary   B. storm
    C. combined   D. constant-flow

KEY (CORRECT ANSWERS)

1.	C	16.	B
2.	A	17.	D
3.	C	18.	C
4.	A	19.	D
5.	C	20.	A
6.	D	21.	C
7.	A	22.	B
8.	C	23.	D
9.	C	24.	D
10.	C	25.	A
11.	B	26.	B
12.	A	27.	D
13.	D	28.	C
14.	A	29.	B
15.	D	30.	A

EXAMINATION SECTION
TEST 1

DIRECTIONS: Each question or incomplete statement is followed by several suggested answers or completions. Select the one that BEST answers the question or completes the statement. *PRINT THE LETTER OF THE CORRECT ANSWER IN THE SPACE AT THE RIGHT.*

1. The Model Cities program, which was authorized by the *Demonstration Cities and Metropolitan Development Act* was designed to

    A. help selected areas plan, administer, and carry out coordinated physical and social programs to improve the environment
    B. aid non-profit organizations to develop and demonstrate new ways of providing housing for low-income families
    C. encourage architects and builders to devise new large-scale construction techniques
    D. offer an alternative to usual urban renewal procedures through funding specific renewal activities on a yearly basis

2. The MAJOR purpose of the capital budgeting process in local government is to

    A. provide operating funds for the various departments
    B. centralize budget decision power in the executive branch
    C. centralize budget decision power in the Council
    D. establish a rational system of priorities for construction

3. The economic base of a community is

    A. the number of wealthy people with annual earnings in excess of $100,000 per year as a ratio to the total population
    B. the percentage of factory employed residents as a ratio of the total work force
    C. the productive industries located within the boundaries of a community
    D. those activities which provide the basic employment and income on which the rest of the local economy depends

4. One of the reasons for the creation of *superagencies* within city government was to

    A. create agencies that would serve as liaisons between the mayor's office and the community
    B. decentralize some of the functions for which the old agencies formerly had responsibility
    C. make each agency autonomous
    D. eliminate duplication of activities among different agencies

5. The word *autonomy* means

    A. automatic
    B. disregard of externals
    C. unlimited power or authority
    D. independent, self-governing

6. De facto, as in de facto segregation, means

   A. by right, in accordance with law
   B. actual
   C. disguised
   D. unintentional

7. American cities gain their legal powers from

   A. the Federal government
   B. the State government
   C. the United States Constitution
   D. common law

8. In an average urban area, the one of the following land uses that would account for the LARGEST percentage of land is

   A. residences   B. streets
   C. business and industry   D. public and semi-public uses

9. A cul-de-sac street is a

   A. dead-end street terminating in a circular turn-around
   B. loop street branching off from a collector street
   C. narrow street which has become congested as the result of commercial development
   D. gridiron street on which through traffic is prohibited

10. In the city, the capital budget is initially prepared by the

    A. city council   B. comptroller
    C. city planning commission   D. budget director

11. Reasonably well-to-do residential communities have joined the search for non-residential taxpayers but have shown LEAST inclination to plan for

    A. the necessary public utilities
    B. adequate access to the sites
    C. housing the workers
    D. the Budget Director

12. The GREATEST percentage of the daytime population of the business center of the city arrives by

    A. railroad   B. subway
    C. bus   D. passenger car

13. The LARGEST single public expenditure in most cities and suburbs in the State is for

    A. schools and education
    B. highways
    C. hospitals and health facilities
    D. police protection

14. The legal basis of zoning is 14.____

    A. the police power
    B. the power to levy taxes
    C. the Federal Constitution
    D. a special act of Congress

15. A drug used in addiction programs as a substitute for heroin is 15.____

    A. benzedrine
    B. librium
    C. methadone
    D. methanimine

16. The STOLcraft is a(n) 16.____

    A. high speed hydrofoil proposed as an alternative to the use of the ferry
    B. vehicle which travels just above the surface of either land or water on a cushion of air
    C. airplane intended for short distance trips between city centers
    D. cargo ship for containerized freight

Questions 17-21.

DIRECTIONS: Questions 17 through 21 are to be answered on the basis of the following information.

FLOOR AREA

Floor area is the sum of the gross areas of the several floors of a building or buildings, measured from the exterior faces of exterior walls or from the center lines of walls separating two buildings.

FLOOR AREA RATIO

Floor area ratio is the total floor area on a zoning lot, divided by the lot area of that zoning lot. (For example, a building containing 20,000 square feet of floor area on a zoning lot of 10,000 square feet has a floor area ratio of 2.0.) Expressed as a formula:

$$FAR = \frac{Floor\ Area}{Lot\ Area}$$

OPEN SPACE RATIO

The *open space ratio* of a zoning lot is the number of square feet of open space on the zoning lot, expressed as a percentage of the floor area on that zoning lot. (For example, if for a particular building an open space ratio of 20 is required, 20,000 square feet of floor area in the building would necessitate 4,000 square feet of open space on the zoning lot upon which the building stands, or, if 6,000 square feet of lot area were in open space, 30,000 square feet of floor area could be in the building on that zoning lot.) Each square foot of open space per 100 square feet of floor area is referred to as one point.
Expressed as a formula:

$$OSR = \frac{100 \times open\ space}{Floor\ Area}$$

17. If a building can be built with a maximum floor area ratio (FAR) of 10.0, this means   17.___

    A. the building can have a maximum of ten stories
    B. the maximum ratio of gross square feet of floor area to area of the first floor is 10:1
    C. that open space on the zoning lot must be provided in an amount equal to ten percent of the total floor area of the building
    D. the maximum ratio of gross square feet of floor area to lot area is 10:1

18. If the open space ratio of a particular building is 18.5 and the actual amount of open space is 13,550 square feet, the floor area of the building must be MOST NEARLY   18.___

    A. 250,675   B. 73,243   C. 28,170   D. 79,027

19. Given: A housing site of 43,560 square feet.   19.___
    At an FAR of 3.33, the allowable total floor area of a proposed building would be MOST NEARLY

    A. 30,736   B. 484,482   C. 48,448   D. 145,055

20. Given: A housing site of 43,560 square feet.   20.___
    At an FAR of 2.94 and an open space ratio of 24.0, how much open space must be provided?

    A. 30,736   B. 10,454   C. 14,816   D. 18,150

21. Given: A housing site of 43,560 square feet.   21.___
    If a proposed building on this site were to have 122,839 gross square feet of floor space, what would the FAR be?

    A. 10.0
    B. 25.5
    C. 2.82
    D. Cannot be determined from data given

Questions 22-24.

DIRECTIONS: Questions 22 through 24 are to be answered on the basis of the following table.

The age characteristics of the total population in a certain neighborhood are as follows:

Age	Number of People
3	2
5	4
12	3
18	3
20	1
21	3
22	4
50	2
56	1
72	2

22. The mean age of the population in the neighborhood described above is MOST NEARLY   22.____

    A. 15   B. 19   C. 23   D. 27

23. The median age of the population in the neighborhood described above is MOST NEARLY   23.____

    A. 15   B. 20   C. 25   D. 30

24. The percentage of the population over age 65 in the neighborhood described above is MOST NEARLY   24.____

    A. 2   B. 4   C. 6   D. 8

25.   25.____

Assume that the above drawing has been made to scale. The total gross floor area of the 20-story tower is, in square feet, MOST NEARLY

    A. 200,000   B. 100,000   C. 1,000   D. 50,000

KEY (CORRECT ANSWERS)

1. A
2. D
3. D
4. D
5. D

6. B
7. B
8. A
9. A
10. C

11. C
12. B
13. A
14. A
15. C

16. C
17. D
18. B
19. D
20. A

21. C
22. C
23. B
24. D
25. A

TEST 2

DIRECTIONS: Each question or incomplete statement is followed by several suggested answers or completions. Select the one that BEST answers the question or completes the statement. *PRINT THE LETTER OF THE CORRECT ANSWER IN THE SPACE AT THE RIGHT.*

1. In the city, the body that is responsible for choosing the specific location of sites for public improvement is the

    A. city planning commission
    B. department of public works
    C. site selection board
    D. fine arts commission

    1.____

2. Publicly-sponsored Early Childhood programs in the city do NOT include

    A. Family Day Care
    B. Headstart Program
    C. playschools for 2- and 3-year olds
    D. pre-kindergarten in elementary schools

    2.____

3. The one of the following that is NOT a current method of controlling pollution is the

    A. requirement that incinerators in the city be upgraded
    B. project for recycling waste paper and aluminum goods for re-use
    C. sale of non-leaded gasoline for automobiles
    D. conversion of all combined sewers in the city to separate sanitary and storm sewers

    3.____

4. In general, the MOST accurate 5-year projection of population can be made for the

    A. nation
    B. metropolitan area
    C. inner city
    D. neighborhood

    4.____

5. The type of area in which the GREATEST percentage increase in population occurred between 1960 and 1980 was in the

    A. central cities
    B. suburban rings
    C. rural non-farm areas
    D. rural farm areas

    5.____

6. The one of the following that should NOT be included in a community planning study undertaken by a city planning department is

    A. a survey of how land is used in the area
    B. compilation of data on school utilization
    C. determination of rent levels in the area
    D. renovation of an old building at rents suitable for low-income people

    6.____

7. The one of the following men who had a role in laying out cities along the formal lines of the *City Beautiful* movement was

    A. Rexford Tugwell
    B. Daniel Burnham
    C. Clarence Stein
    D. Frank Lloyd Wright

    7.____

65

8. A key factor leading to the development of suburban growth in recent decades is

   A. a series of regional government compacts
   B. the large increase in automobile ownership
   C. the drying up of immigration
   D. the gradual shifting of some shopping and employment from the center of the city to the outskirts

9. A controlled aerial mosaic photograph would be LEAST useful in which of the following types of planning work?

   A. Land use study of undeveloped land
   B. Review of subdivision plats
   C. Study of proposed highway locations
   D. Building condition study of CBD

10. The MAJOR function of the city community planning boards is

    A. to prepare capital and expense budgets for community planning districts
    B. to advise the county executives and city agencies on planning issues
    C. as an umbrella organization for local poverty groups
    D. to provide technical planning help to local community groups

11. Special revenue sharing is intended to

    A. be available only for cities of over 1 million population
    B. be available for general purpose use, to be determined by the cities
    C. replace money previously distributed to cities for categorical grants
    D. in all instances be passed from the state to the city

12. The city's water pollution control plants are being upgraded to _____ treatment which removes _____.

    A. primary; "approximately" 65% of pollutants
    B. secondary; approximately 90% of pollutants
    C. tertiary; approximately 99% of pollutants
    D. desalination; all the mineral matter

13. *Turnkey* housing refers to

    A. a method of housing construction whereby a private developer finances and constructs the housing to the city's standards and the housing is then purchased by the city
    B. the conversion of old-law housing to co-op housing in moderate rent areas, including rent subsidies for low-income families
    C. brownstone renovation with no public subsidy in historic districts where the design must be approved by the landmarks commission
    D. a form of mixing housing with commercial or industrial space, as in the incentive zoning amendment

14. The Planned-Unit Development is a provision of the city zoning resolution which 14.____

    A. provides for industrial development on the outskirts of the city
    B. requires the building of schools, community centers, and shopping facilities as part of a large residential development
    C. permits housing to be built close together in clusters, leaving substantial land areas in their natural state as common open spaces
    D. provides a means of constructing off-street parking facilities in high density residential neighborhoods

15. The official map differs from the master plan in that it 15.____

    A. deals only with proposed streets as they relate to existing streets
    B. includes a detailed engineering design for the existing and proposed street system
    C. is an accurate description of the location of public improvements existing and proposed
    D. is tied directly to the Capital Budget and Improvement Program

16. According to the zoning resolution, a legal non-conforming use in zoning is one established 16.____

    A. prior to the adoption of the ordinance provision prohibiting it
    B. by a special exception permit issued by the planning commission
    C. by a variance issued by the board of standards and appeals
    D. for many years despite the prohibition in the ordinance and which had not been proceeded against

17. The formula for financing interstate highways under state and Federal law provides that the government of the city shall pay what percent of the cost of highway construction? 17.____

    A. 100%   B. 90%   C. 40%   D. 0%

18. The one of the following statements that MOST NEARLY expresses the city's long-term program in regard to arterial highways is to 18.____

    A. provide many routes throughout the city in order to minimize travel time from all points
    B. provide quick vehicular access from the business center to the suburbs
    C. build up bypass routes to discourage traffic from entering the business center
    D. build up the highway network in the outer boroughs and to landbank land in the business center for future through routes

19. The city planning commission 19.____

    A. consists of lifetime members, who annually elect a chairman
    B. administers the zoning resolution and hears appeals for variances
    C. prepares the annual 5-year capital improvement plan
    D. prepares the architectural designs for all public buildings, except schools

20. The feature of the city zoning resolution before 1961 which gave the city's skyscrapers their MOST distinctive architectural character was its   20.___

    A. height bonus for added setbacks
    B. rear yard provisions
    C. off-street parking and loading requirements
    D. density restrictions

KEY (CORRECT ANSWERS)

1.	C	11.	C
2.	C	12.	B
3.	D	13.	A
4.	A	14.	C
5.	B	15.	A
6.	D	16.	A
7.	B	17.	D
8.	B	18.	C
9.	D	19.	C
10.	B	20.	A

TEST 3

DIRECTIONS: Each question or incomplete statement is followed by several suggested answers or completions. Select the one that BEST answers the question or completes the statement. *PRINT THE LETTER OF THE CORRECT ANSWER IN THE SPACE AT THE RIGHT.*

Questions 1-3.

DIRECTIONS: Questions 1 through 3, inclusive, are to be answered in accordance with the following paragraphs.

Into the nine square miles that make up Manhattan's business districts, about two million people travel each weekday to go to work — the equivalent of the combined populations of Boston, Baltimore, and Cincinnati. Some 140,000 drive there in cars, 200,000 take buses, and 100,000 ride the commuter railroads. The great majority, however, go by subway — approximately 1.4 million people.

It is some ride. The last major improvement in the subway system was completed in 1935. The subways are dirty and noisy. Many local lines operate well beneath capacity; but many express lines are strained way beyond capacity in particular, the lines to Manhattan, now overloaded by 39,000 passengers during peak hours.

But for all its discomforts, the subway system is inherently a far more efficient way of moving people than automobiles and highways. Making this system faster, more convenient, and more comfortable for people must be the core of the city's transportation effort.

1. The CENTRAL point of the above text is that

   A. the equivalent of the combined populations of Boston, Baltimore, and Cincinnati commute into Manhattan's business district each weekday
   B. the improvement of the subway system is the key to the solution of moving people efficiently in and out of Manhattan's business district
   C. the subways are dirty and noisy, resulting in a terrible ride
   D. we should increase the ability of people to get in and out of Manhattan by cars, subways, and commuter railroads in order to ease the load from the subways

2. In accordance with the above paragraphs, 1.4 million people commute by subway and _____ by other mass transportation means.

   A. 200,000   B. 100,000   C. 440,000   D. 300,000

3. From the information given in the above paragraphs, one could logically conclude that, next to the subways, the transportation system that carries the LARGEST number of passengers is (the)

   A. railroads   B. cars
   C. buses   D. local lines

Questions 4-6.

DIRECTIONS: Questions 4 through 6, inclusive, are to be answered in accordance with the following paragraphs.

Incentive zoning is an affirmative tool that has widespread applications. The Zoning Resolution which became effective in 1981 substantially reduced the amount of floor space that a developer could put up on a given size lot and increased the light and air. In the Chrysler Building, which was built under the old legislation, the floor space is 27 times the size of the lot. The maximum ratio allowed for buildings now without a special permit is 18.

The newer zoning ordinance provided incentives to developers to devote part of the plot to public plazas or arcades. This space is needed to supplement the sidewalks, which in many cases are as narrow as they were when the midtown area was lined with brownstone or brickfront houses.

While the newer zoning has produced plazas, it has not of itself proved to be a sufficient development control. Stretches of Third Avenue and the Avenue of the Americas, for example, have been almost completely redeveloped in the last few years. This massive private investment has produced several fine individual buildings. The total environment produced, however, has been disappointing in a number of respects, and there is nowhere near the amenity that there could have been.

4. According to the paragraphs above, the use of incentive zoning has not been entirely successful because it has

   A. discouraged redevelopment
   B. encouraged massive private development along Third Avenue
   C. been ineffective in controlling overall redevelopment
   D. not significantly increased the number of parks and plazas being built

5. According to the above paragraphs, one might conclude that before the new Zoning Resolution was passed,

   A. buildings on a given site were required to have greater setbacks
   B. the amount of private investment in development was significantly smaller than it is today
   C. no controls on development existed
   D. the provision of parks and plazas was less frequent

6. In the context of the above paragraphs, the word *amenity* means

   A. compliance with regulations
   B. correction of undesirable environmental aspects
   C. responsiveness to guidelines and incentives
   D. pleasant or desirable features

Questions 7-8.

DIRECTIONS: Questions 7 and 8 are to be answered in accordance with the following paragraphs.

We must also find better ways to handle the relocation of people uprooted by projects. In the past, many renewal plans have foundered on this problem, and it is still the most difficult part of community development. Large-scale replacement of low-income residents — many ineligible for public housing — has contributed to deterioration of surrounding communities, as in Manhattan's West Side, Coney Island, and Arverne. Recently, thanks to changes in Housing Authority procedures, relocation has been accomplished in a far more satisfactory fashion. The step-by-step community development projects we advocate in this plan should bring further improvement.

But additional measures will be necessary. There are going to be more people to be moved; and, with the current shortage of apartments, large ones especially, it is going to be tougher to find places to move them to. The city should have more freedom to buy or lease housing that comes on the market because of normal turnover and make it available to relocatees.

7. According to the above paragraphs, one of the reasons a neighborhood may deteriorate is that

    A. there is a scarcity of large apartments
    B. step-by-step community development projects have failed
    C. people in the given neighborhood are uprooted from their homes
    D. a nearby renewal project has an inadequate relocation plan

7.____

8. From the above paragraphs, one might conclude that the relocation phase of community renewal has been improved

    A. by changes in Housing Authority procedures
    B. by development of step-by-step community development projects
    C. through expanded city powers to buy housing for relocation
    D. through the Housing Authority Leasing Program

8.____

Questions 9-10.

DIRECTIONS: Questions 9 and 10 are to be answered in accordance with the following paragraphs.

Provision of decent housing for the lower half of the population (by income) was thus taken on as a public responsibility. Public housing was to assist the poorest quarter of urban families while the 221(d)(3) Housing Program would assist the next quarter. But limited funds meant that the supply of subsidized housing could not stretch nearly far enough to help this half of the population. Who were to be left out in the rationing process which was accomplished by the sifting of applicants for housing on the part of public and private authorities?

Discrimination on the grounds of race or color is not allowed under Federal law. In all sections of the country, encouragingly, housing programs are found which allow this law to the letter. Yet, housing programs in some cities still suffer from the residue of racial segregation policies and attitudes that for years were condoned or even encouraged.

Some sifting in the 221(d)(3) Housing Program follows the practice of many public housing authorities, the imposition of requirements with respect to character. This is a delicate matter. To fill a project overwhelmingly with broken families, alcoholics, criminals, delinquents, and other problem tenants would hardly make it a wholesome environment. Yet the total exclusion of such families is hardly an acceptable alternative. To the extent this exclusion is practiced, the very people whose lives are described in order to persuade lawmakers and the public to instigate new programs find the door shut in their faces when such programs come into being. The proper balance is difficult to achieve, but society's neediest families surely should not be totally denied the opportunities for rejuvenation in subsidized housing.

9. From the above paragraphs, it can be assumed that the 221(d)(3) Housing Program

   A. served a population earning more than the median income
   B. served a less affluent population than is served by public housing
   C. excludes all problem families from its projects
   D. is a subsidized housing program

10. According to the above paragraphs, the provision of housing for the poor

    A. has not been completely accomplished with public monies
    B. is never influenced by segregationist policies
    C. is limited to providing housing for only the neediest families
    D. is primarily the responsibility of the Federal government

Questions 11-12.

DIRECTIONS: Questions 11 and 12 are to be answered in accordance with the following paragraph.

Though the recent trend toward apartment construction may appear to be the region's response to large-lot zoning and centralized industry, it really is not. It is mainly a function of the age of the population (coupled with a rush to build apartments in the city between the passage of the newer zoning ordinance and its enforcement in December 1981). Most of the apartments are occupied by one- and two-person families — young people out of school but without a family of their own and older people whose children have grown. Both groups have been increasing in number; and, in this region, they characteristically live in apartments. It is this increased demand for apartments and the simultaneous decrease in demand for one-family houses that dramatically raised the percentage of building permits issued for multi-family housing units from 36 percent in 1977 to 67 percent in 1981. The fact that three-fourths of the apartments were built in the Core between 1977 and 1981 at the same time as the Core was losing population underscores the failure of the apartment boom to slow the outward spread of the population.

11. According to the above paragraph, one of the reasons for the increase in the number of building permits issued for multi-family construction in the city metropolitan region is

    A. that workers in industry want to live close to their jobs
    B. an increase in the number of elderly people living in the region
    C. the inability of many families to afford the large lots necessary to build private homes
    D. the new zoning ordinance made it easier to build apartments

12. According to the above paragraph, the apartment construction boom

    A. increased the population density in the core
    B. spurred a population shift to the suburbs
    C. did not halt the outward flow of the population from the core
    D. was most significant in the outer areas of the region

Questions 13-14.

DIRECTIONS: Questions 13 and 14 are to be answered in accordance with the following paragraphs.

The city's economy has its own dynamics, and there is only so much the government can do to shape it. But that margin is critically important. If the city uses its points of leverage, it can generate a large number of jobs and good jobs, jobs that lead to advancement.

As a major employer itself, the city can upgrade the jobs it offers and greatly improve its services to the public if it does so. Since highly skilled professionals will always be in short supply, the city must train more paraprofessionals to take over routine tasks. Equally important, it must provide them with a realistic job ladder so they can move on up — nurse's aide to certified nurse, for example, teacher's aide to teacher. The training programs for such upgrading will require a substantial public investment but the cost-benefit return should be excellent.

As a major purchaser of goods and services, the city can stimulate business enterprise in the ghetto. The growth of Black and Puerto Rican firms will produce more local jobs; it will also create the kind of managerial talent the ghetto needs.

New kinds of enterprise can be set up. In housing, for example, there is a huge backlog of rehabilitation work to be done and a large pool of unskilled manpower to be trained for it. Corporations can be formed to take over tenements, remodel, maintain, and operate them, as in the Brownsville Home Maintenance Program. Grocery cooperatives to bring food prices down are another possibility.

13. According to the above paragraphs, the city is the major employer and, by using its capacity, it can

   A. assist unskilled people with talent to move up on the job ladder
   B. create private enterprises that will renew all areas of the city in need of renewal
   C. eliminate poverty in the ghetto areas by selective purchase of goods and services
   D. have no influence on the economy of the city

14. According to the above paragraphs, one may REASONABLY conclude that

   A. the city has no power to influence the job market
   B. a by-product of strategic purchasing and employment and training practices can be the rehabilitation of housing and the lowering of food prices
   C. highly skilled professions, which are now in short supply, will no longer be needed after paraprofessionals are trained to take over routine jobs
   D. the city's major objective is to bring down food prices

15. 500 persons attended a public hearing at which a proposed public housing project was being considered. Less than half favored the project, while the majority opposed the project.
    According to the above statement, it is REASONABLE to conclude that

   A. the proposal stimulated considerable community interest
   B. the public housing project was disapproved by the city because a majority opposed it

C. those who opposed the project lacked sympathy for needy persons
D. the supporters of the project were led by militants

16. A document was published by a public agency and distributed for discussion. The document contained data showing trends in the level of reading among freshmen college students and suggested that the high schools were not investing enough effort in overcoming retardation. It compared the costs of intensifying reading instruction in the secondary schools as compared to costs in college for such instruction.
According to the above statement, it is REASONABLE to conclude that

   A. the document proposed new programs
   B. the college students read better than high school students
   C. some college students need remedial reading
   D. the study was done by a consultant

17. A vacant lot close to a polluted creek is for sale. Two buyers compete. One owns an adjacent factory which provides 300 high paying unskilled jobs. He needs to expand or move from the city. If he expands, he will provide 300 additional jobs. The other is a community group in a changing residential area close by. They hope to stabilize the neighborhood by bringing in new housing. They could build an apartment building with 100 dwelling units on the lot.
According to the above paragraph, it is REASONABLE to conclude that

   A. jobs are more important than housing
   B. there is conflict between the factory owners and the neighborhood group
   C. the neighborhood group will not succeed in stabilizing the area by constructing new housing
   D. the polluted creek should be cleaned up

Questions 18-21.

DIRECTIONS: Questions 18 through 21, inclusive, refer to the phrases shown below. For each of the questions, select that phrase which BEST completes the sentence for that question.

   A. to increase training and educational opportunities
   B. to remove social ills by a slum clearance program
   C. to select the goals and values to which these resources should be directed
   D. to diminish drastic redevelopment, to provide opportunities to move within the area, or to move to new areas which can be assimilated to old objectives

18. In addition to concern with the rational allocation of resources, the urban planning process needs _____.

19. The early housing reformers emphasized the inadequate physical environment of the slums, understressed the connection between the social environment of the slums and the disorders they wanted to cure, and attempted _____.

20. The objective for assisting the transition to middle class status will mean intensified efforts _____.   20.____

21. To provide a sense of continuity for those people whose residential areas are being renewed, mainly working class, it is desirable _____.   21.____

Questions 22-25.

DIRECTIONS: For Questions 22 through 25, select that item from Column B that is MOST closely related to the item in Column A.

COLUMN A	COLUMN B	
22. City Map	A. Citizen Participation	22.____
23. Revenue Sharing	B. Block Grants	23.____
24. Opportunity Structure	C. Streets	24.____
25. Public Hearing	D. Upward Mobility	25.____

KEY (CORRECT ANSWERS)

1. B		11. B	
2. D		12. C	
3. C		13. A	
4. C		14. B	
5. D		15. A	
6. D		16. C	
7. D		17. B	
8. A		18. C	
9. D		19. B	
10. A		20. A	

21. D
22. C
23. B
24. D
25. A

EXAMINATION SECTION
TEST 1

DIRECTIONS: Each question or incomplete statement is followed by several suggested answers or completions. Select the one that BEST answers the question or completes the statement. *PRINT THE LETTER OF THE CORRECT ANSWER IN THE SPACE AT THE RIGHT.*

1. Ebenezer Howard is BEST known for the concept of self-sufficient towns with mixed economies which are called

   A. new towns
   B. garden cities
   C. planned unit developments
   D. suburbs

   1._____

2. The new town of Columbia, Maryland, has which of the following planned features?
   I. Neighborhood clusters
   II. A rail commuter system
   III. Prior land assembly
   IV. Prohibition of industry
   The CORRECT answer is:

   A. II only   B. I, III   C. II, IV   D. I, III, IV

   2._____

3. The two lines on the graph shown at the right BEST represent which of the following combinations of travel behavior in a metropolitan area of 2 million population?

   A. Transit and private automobile trips
   B. Weekday and weekend trips
   C. All work and nonwork trips
   D. Office and retail-generated trips

   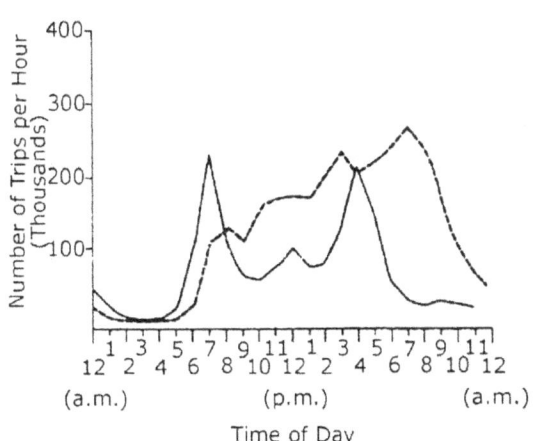

   3._____

4. Assume that you are the director of a local planning agency, and that you recognize the interdependency of the chief executive, the planning agency, operating departments, and independent boards and commissions. In a hypothetical situation, a proposed expansion of a county airport and adjacent industrial areas is in opposition to the planning agency's proposal for a regional park location.
   The planning agency believes there are unique circumstances and sound reasons for preferring the regional park proposal along with future relocation of the airport to another site in the county.
   Which of the following strategies would likely place you, as the planning director, in the LEAST effective coordinating role in resolving the conflict?

   4._____

A. Attempting to have the planning agency solely responsible for additional studies and recommendations
B. Directing planning staff to discontinue all studies of this issue and direct all inquiries regarding this matter to the director
C. Recommending the study control be given to the staff of the chief executive's office
D. Soliciting support of other departments and agencies for the planning agency's regional park proposal

5. Recent major developments in household characteristics in the United States have been characterized by which of the following?
   I. A marked increase in nonfamily living arrangements among the adult population has been observed in recent years.
   II. A major development in marriage trends has been the sharply decreasing level of divorce in central cities.
   III. Families (households where all members are related) maintained by either men or women who have no spouse living with them represent a growing proportion of all family households.
   IV. After several decades of decline in household size, the number of persons per unit has increased in metropolitan area since 1970.

   The CORRECT answer is:

   A. I only   B. I, III   C. III, IV   D. I, II, IV

Questions 6-9.

DIRECTIONS: The group of questions below consists of four lettered headings followed by a list of numbered phrases. For each numbered phrase, select the one heading which is MOST closely related to it. One heading may be used once, more than once, or not at all.

In the following list, which of the formal bodies that operate within a city most likely would take final action on each of the following requests?

   A. City Council
   B. City Court
   C. Board of Zoning Appeals
   D. School Board

6. A request to acquire land for a new school.

7. A request to condemn property in a blighted area.

8. A request to levy a special property assessment for a street.

9. A request for a variance from a zoning ordinance.

10. In reference to the following hypothetical linear regression equation that describes household trip generation with the census tract as the unit of analysis, which of the following statements about R^2 is CORRECT?

   $T = -.65 + .96(p) + .61(v)$
   $R^2 = .69$
   T = the average number of daily vehicle trips from home per DU (dwelling unit)
   p = persons per DU
   v = vehicles per DU

   A. It shows that more p causes households to make more trips.
   B. It shows that more p, only when coupled with more automobiles, causes households to make more trips.
   C. It indicates that 69% of the variation in trip generation is explained by p and v.
   D. There is a 45% probability that the variables T, p, and v are correlated by chance.

10._____

Questions 11-14.

DIRECTIONS: Questions 11 through 14 are to be answered on the basis of the following circumstance.

The desirability and feasibility of a proposed shopping center are to be evaluated. The primary concerns are that conditions of the city zoning ordinance be met and that the project be a profitable venture. The developer owns a 30-acre parcel and proposes to construct a 250,000-square foot leasable area with 1,300 on-site parking spaces. The shopping center will serve a trade area that contains 20,000 households. The average household disposable income is $12,000. The shopping center will have a 50:50 split of square footage between convenience and shopper's goods.

11. Which of the following would be APPROPRIATE in a shopping center of this size?

   A. A major grocery and a drugstore as prime tenants
   B. Either a department or discount store as the anchor tenant
   C. Three department stores of approximately the same size
   D. A series of smaller stores rather than an anchor tenant

11._____

12. If an average of 400 square feet is needed to accommodate each parking space and associated driveways, the APPROXIMATE acreage of the blacktop area of the site would be _____ acres.

   A. Less than 10
   B. Between 10 and 15
   C. Between 15 and 20
   D. More than 20

12._____

13. If 50 percent of disposable income is allocated to retail purchases, a minimum of $100 of sales per square foot is needed to operate profitably, and 750,000 square feet of retail business already exists in the trade area, which of the following should be concluded? The

   A. trade area is already overbuilt and cannot support additional development without further population growth
   B. new shopping center will use up all of the untapped purchasing power of the trade area

13._____

4 (#1)

C. existing and proposed centers can operate profitably with excess purchasing power available for additional development
D. trade area is not overbuilt presently, but it can only accommodate an additional 150,000 square feet

14. Provisions in the zoning ordinance require a 4:1 ratio of open space to building space and a 5:1,000-square foot ratio of parking space to gross leasable area (GLA). According to the ordinance, which of the following statements about the parcel is CORRECT?
It is

    A. too small to accommodate the projected center, although adequate parking would be provided
    B. large enough to accommodate the projected center, but parking spaces would be inadequate
    C. large enough to accommodate the projected center, and sufficient parking would be provided
    D. grossly underutilized and could accommodate additional square footage and additional parking spaces

14.____

Questions 15-17.

DIRECTIONS: Questions 15 through 17 are to be answered on the basis of the following information.

Planners in a large city that consists of 150 neighborhoods are concerned about the provision and allocation of health-care clinics at the multiple-neighborhood level throughout the city. One of the main concerns is prenatal health care. Variables relevant to this situation are as follows:

    QPNHC = the overall quality of prenatal health care
    IMR = the percentage of children who survive their first three months of life (a type of infant mortality rate) and who were born in the same one-year period
    NWP = the number of women pregnant at any time during a one-year period
    NA = the number of appointments kept at the health clinic per year
    FI = the family incomes of residents in thousands of dollars ($1,000's)
    D = the distance of families from the health clinics in miles

(Neighborhood averages can be generated for each of these variables.)

15. The planners have decided that the neighborhood infant mortality rate will serve as the operational objective of the prenatal health care system.
Which of the following would be the MOST serious criticism leveled against their decision?

    A. It is impossible to calculate the IMR at the neighborhood level.
    B. The data on the use of the clinic (NA) are easier to obtain and more accurate than the other data.
    C. The IMR is a good quantitative but weak qualitative index of the QPNHC.
    D. The collection of IMR data is irrelevant to the problem.

15.____

16. Which of the following is an output variable within the model?

    A. IMR   B. NWP   C. FI   D. D

16.____

17. It is now 10 years later; the clinics were built and a very comprehensive data collection system was kept in operation. The clinic programs are under fire, the budgets are expected to be slashed, and some clinics probably will be forced to close. Time is short. Based on this situation, which of the following would be the LEAST critical evaluation question?

   A. Are higher levels of clinic usage associated with various infant mortality rates?
   B. If distance does not affect the use of the clinics, does it do so differentially by income strata?
   C. What kinds of persons (education, income level, etc.) use each clinic?
   D. Are family income levels associated with distance

17.____

KEY (CORRECT ANSWERS)

1. B
2. B
3. C
4. B
5. B

6. D
7. A
8. A
9. C
10. C

11. B
12. B
13. C
14. C
15. C
16. A
17. D

EXAMINATION SECTION
TEST 1

DIRECTIONS: Each question or incomplete statement is followed by several suggested, answers or completions. Select the one that BEST answers the question or completes the statement. *PRINT THE LETTER OF THE CORRECT ANSWER IN THE SPACE AT THE RIGHT.*

1. The authority to establish zoning ordinances by a community comes from

    A. the police power of the state
    B. local determination
    C. the federal government
    D. implied powers of the community

    1._____

2. On a land use map, the standard color used to designate residential use is

    A. green   B. blue   C. purple   D. yellow

    2._____

3. In population analysis, a population pyramid indicates

    A. male and female age groupings
    B. total population projections
    C. fertility ratios
    D. educational achievements

    3._____

4. The determination of a standard metropolitan statistical area is established by

    A. local considerations   B. regional agencies
    C. the U.S. Census Bureau   D. state agencies

    4._____

5. The population census of the United States is taken every _____ years.

    A. 2   B. 4   C. 5   D. 10

    5._____

6. There are strong indications that planning agencies are developing a new approach to the traditional methods of city planning.
   This new approach is called

    A. advocacy planning
    B. long-range physical planning
    C. community development
    D. policies planning

    6._____

7. A key element of a comprehensive plan for a community is the

    A. zoning ordinance   B. land use plan
    C. official map   D. subdivision regulation

    7._____

8. The official map of a community is a document that

    A. shows population projections and educational trends
    B. pinpoints the location of future streets and other public facilities
    C. identifies capital improvements and budgets
    D. indicates all community facilities

    8._____

83

9. During the past decade, planning programs generally have become increasingly concerned with which one of the following?

   A. Long-range physical design
   B. Highway locations
   C. Social welfare
   D. Natural resources

10. The city planning process encompasses several basic phases. Which one of the following phases would NOT be considered typical?

    A. Cost-benefit analysis
    B. Goal formulation
    C. Data collection and research
    D. Plan preparation and programming

11. The MOST common use of easements in new housing subdivisions is for

    A. air rights   B. utilities
    C. open space   D. absorption fields

12. The phrase *non-complying use* relates to which one of the following regulations?

    A. Zoning Ordinance   B. Building Code
    C. Subdivision regulations D. Health Code

13. Performance standards are generally associated with which one of the following types of zoning districts?

    A. Residential   B. Commercial
    C. Manufacturing   D. Flood plain

14. The PRIMARY goal of cluster-type development is to

    A. increase population density
    B. insure open space
    C. discourage rapid development
    D. bypass zoning requirements

15. Which of the following is MOST closely related to the land-use intensity standards developed by the Federal Housing Administration?

    A. Quality of housing   B. Planned unit development
    C. Low-cost housing   D. Land management policy

16. If the density of a residential subdivision is 8 dwelling units per acre, then the average size lot should be APPROXIMATELY

    A. 25 ft. x 100 ft.   B. 55 ft. x 100 ft.
    C. 100 ft. x 100 ft.   D. 200 ft. x 200 ft.

17. In planning the open parking area for community facilities, the amount of space allocated per care should be APPROXIMATELY _____ sq.ft.

    A. 150   B. 300   C. 600   D. 800

18. Which of the following facilities would be MOST appropriate on the roof of a building?

    A. Stolport
    B. Heliport
    C. Airport
    D. Cargo port

19. Sanitary landfill is a method of

    A. sewage disposal
    B. composting
    C. incineration
    D. refuse disposal

20. Which of the following is NOT considered to be an air pollutant by the Environmental Protection Agency?

    A. Nitrates
    B. Sulfur oxides
    C. Carbon monoxide
    D. Hydrocarbons

21. Which of the following recreation facilities is NOT considered a typical neighborhood facility?

    A. Tot lot
    B. Playground
    C. Wading pool
    D. Playfield

22. Which of the following methods would be the MOST accurate in making a population projection for a small community?

    A. Migration and natural increase
    B. Apportionment and voting records
    C. School enrollment and housing starts
    D. Geometric extrapolation

23. When a planning map is to be reproduced to different sizes, the map scale should be expressed

    A. mathematically
    B. in graphic form
    C. in feet and inches
    D. by metes and bounds

24. The one of the following characteristics which is NOT typical of new industrial parks is

    A. off-street loading
    B. extensive landscaping
    C. employee parking
    D. 2-story structures

25. A greenbelt surrounding a community can be used for many activities. The one of the following activities LEAST appropriate for greenbelt use is

    A. farming
    B. recreation
    C. local shopping
    D. flood plain control

KEY (CORRECT ANSWERS)

1. A
2. D
3. A
4. C
5. D

6. D
7. B
8. B
9. C
10. A

11. B
12. A
13. C
14. B
15. B

16. B
17. B
18. B
19. D
20. A

21. D
22. A
23. B
24. D
25. C

TEST 2

DIRECTIONS: Each question or incomplete statement is followed by several suggested answers or completions. Select the one that BEST answers the question or completes the statement. *PRINT THE LETTER OF THE CORRECT ANSWER IN THE SPACE AT THE RIGHT.*

1. The *neighborhood unit* concept does NOT provide for   1.____

   A. elementary schools
   B. playgrounds
   C. local shopping
   D. industrial development

2. Which of the following areas is LEAST likely to be considered part of social welfare planning?   2.____

   A. Urban design
   B. Education
   C. Health
   D. Anti-poverty

3. Both the census of business and the census of manufacturing compiled by the U.S. Bureau of the Census are made every _____ years.   3.____

   A. three   B. five   C. seven   D. ten

4. The MOST frequently used governmental source for topographical maps is the U.S.   4.____

   A. Department of Agriculture
   B. Geological Survey
   C. Department of Housing and Urban Development
   D. Coast Guard

5. The importance of assessed valuation of land and buildings to a community is to   5.____

   A. establish school taxes
   B. establish property taxes
   C. determine tax exemptions
   D. determine land uses

6. Of the following countries, the MOST extensive progress in establishing new towns during the 20th century has taken place in   6.____

   A. the United States
   B. France
   C. Italy
   D. England

7. A street classification system is PRIMARILY used for street   7.____

   A. naming
   B. construction
   C. differentiation
   D. location

8. The *Greenbelt* towns were a product of the   8.____

   A. city beautiful movement
   B. garden city movement
   C. atomic energy commission
   D. resettlement administration

87

9. The apportionment method of population projection is concerned PRIMARILY with

   A. migration
   B. natural increase
   C. large geographic areas
   D. birth rate

10. Under ideal conditions, which type of parking arrangement should yield the MOST parking spaces?

    A. Parallel   B. 45°   C. 60°   D. 90°

11. A MAJOR disadvantage of a depressed highway through a built-up area as compared to a highway on grade is its

    A. poor appearance
    B. inadequate width of right-of-way
    C. lack of access
    D. noise generation

12. The customary test made to determine the ability of a soil to drain off liquids, such as those discharged by a cesspool, is known as the _____ test.

    A. percolation
    B. absorption
    C. drainage
    D. sump

13. The Mitchell-Lama Housing Law was originally intended to assist the construction of

    A. low-income housing
    B. middle-income housing
    C. suburban residential projects
    D. housing for mixed racial communities

14. A community will MOST frequently acquire the development rights of existing farm land in order to

    A. protect land values
    B. provide sites for public projects
    C. insure open space
    D. develop a land bank

15. In recent years, local participation in the city planning process has *substantially* increased because of the

    A. establishment of local school boards
    B. high crime rate in the streets
    C. emergence of private citizen organizations
    D. establishment of community planning boards

16. A unique feature of the State Urban Development Corporation when first established was that it

    A. was an autonomous organization
    B. was not required to conform to local zoning regulations
    C. could only build housing when invited by local communities
    D. used only private funds for its projects

17. The concept of *defensible space* has recently emerged to help fight crime in urban areas. The principle of *defensible space* is that public areas should be

    A. completely enclosed
    B. eliminated
    C. placed adjacent to areas of activity
    D. patroled by volunteer citizen groups

17.____

18. Of the following, the MAJOR planning implication of a 3-bedroom dwelling unit as compared to a 1-bedroom dwelling unit is that

    A. the family with the larger dwelling unit has more income
    B. with larger dwelling units there will be fewer municipal services necessary
    C. more children will be enrolled in school
    D. smaller dwelling units are cheaper to build than larger units

18.____

19. A landscaped buffer strip is MOST appropriately placed between which of the following land uses?

    A. Light and heavy manufacturing
    B. Residential and commercial
    C. Commercial and manufacturing
    D. Residential of low density and residential of high density

19.____

20. The employment trend in the city over the past 20 years has shown that

    A. *both* white collar and blue collar jobs have increased
    B. *both* white collar and blue collar jobs have decreased
    C. *only* white collar jobs have decreased
    D. *only* blue collar jobs have decreased

20.____

21. For traffic safety, the BEST angle between two intersecting streets is

    A. 15   B. 30   C. 45   D. 90

21.____

22. In the city, the system used by the tax department to identify property is by

    A. house numbers   B. zoning maps
    C. block and lot numbers   D. the official city map

22.____

23. The name of the report by which the U.S. Environmental Protection Agency establishes the effect of a proposed project on the environment is called the

    A. input-output analysis   B. economic base study
    C. ambient air study   D. impact statement

23.____

24. Planners recommend that utility lines be located underground because utility lines built this way are

    A. cheaper to construct
    B. not required to follow street alignments
    C. aesthetically more attractive
    D. more efficient

24.____

25. *Scatter-site* housing means that the housing will be 25.____
    A. located in all use districts
    B. built with large areas of recreation space between buildings
    C. of different heights on each site
    D. built on small, by-passed sites in built-up areas

KEY (CORRECT ANSWERS)

1. D
2. A
3. B
4. B
5. B

6. D
7. C
8. D
9. C
10. D

11. C
12. A
13. B
14. C
15. D

16. B
17. C
18. C
19. B
20. D

21. D
22. C
23. D
24. C
25. D

EXAMINATION SECTION
TEST 1

DIRECTIONS: Each question or incomplete statement is followed by several suggested answers or completions. Select the one that BEST answers the question or completes the Statement. *PRINT THE LETTER OF THE CORRECT ANSWER IN THE SPACE AT THE RIGHT.*

1. City planning should aim at

    A. over-all planning
    B. administrative planning
    C. planning of only physical facilities
    D. planning of resources

2. The director of planning of a local planning agency is *usually* responsible to the

    A. planning commission   B. city council
    C. mayor   D. city manager

3. The official map is subject to change ONLY by the

    A. planning commission   B. city engineer
    C. legislative body   D. mayor

4. An official map of a city is generally adopted by, and can ONLY be changed by action of the

    A. city engineer   B. planning board
    C. legislative body   D. zoning board of appeals

5. Zoning regulations are generally administered by the

    A. building department   B. planning commission
    C. zoning board of appeals   D. planning director

6. Logical extent of area which should be included in basic studies for a comprehensive city plan is

    A. entire residential area
    B. the neighborhood
    C. area bounded by city boundaries
    D. urban region

7. The safest angle (in degrees) for the intersection of two local streets is

    A. 45   B. 60   C. 90   D. 120

8. The city-beautiful movement is *usually* associated with work of

    A. L'Enfant   B. Burnham   C. Wright   D. Howard

9. The garden city movement is *usually* associated with

    A. Adams   B. Moses   C. Dahir   D. Howard

10. The power to permit variances to the zoning resolution is *usually* vested in the

   A. City Planning Commission
   B. Building Department
   C. City Council
   D. Board of Standards and Appeals

11. "Multiple Dwelling Law" is a

   A. federal law
   B. state law
   C. municipal ordinance
   D. law to protect landlords and hotels

12. The BEST map to use in planning a street layout for a new development is

   A. topographic
   B. planimetric
   C. photo-mosaic
   D. hydrographic chart

13. MAXIMUM auto traffic carrying capacity of a city street is attained at approximate speed of _____ M.P.H.

   A. 10-15   B. 15-25   C. 25-40   D. 40-55

14. A decelerating lane would *most likely* be used in conjunction with a

   A. bridge approach
   B. highway exit
   C. sharp curve on a highway
   D. steep grade on a highway

15. Use of curved streets in suburban development is *desirable* because it

   A. increases sight-distance for motorists
   B. makes a lot layout simpler
   C. forces motorists to reduce speed
   D. reduces surveying costs

16. The LEAST important requirement for a fire hydrant is

   A. accessibility
   B. artistic design
   C. frost proof
   D. mechanical reliability

17. In general, the *highest* tax return per acre of developed land is

   A. business
   B. industry
   C. apartments
   D. single family homes

18. The percentage of developed land area in a city normally taken up by the street system is about _____ %.

   A. 15   B. 25   C. 35   D. 45

19. The greatest amount of land in Manhattan is used for

   A. residences
   B. stores
   C. offices
   D. industry

20. The three "Greenbelt" towns in the United States after World War II were built by   20.____
    A. private capital
    B. the F.H.A.
    C. the Resettlement Administration
    D. the Department of Agriculture

KEY (CORRECT ANSWERS)

1.	A	11.	B
2.	A	12.	A
3.	C	13.	B
4.	C	14.	B
5.	A	15.	C
6.	D	16.	B
7.	C	17.	A
8.	B	18.	C
9.	D	19.	A
10.	D	20.	C

TEST 2

DIRECTIONS: Each question consists of a statement. You are to indicate whether the statement is TRUE (T) or FALSE (F). *PRINT THE LETTER OF THE CORRECT ANSWER IN THE SPACE AT THE RIGHT.*

1. In an *ideal plan,* radial express highways should lead to and through the downtown business center of a city. 1.____

2. In an ideal city plan for a large city, there should be circumferential transit lines NOT giving direct service to the central business district. 2.____

3. Modern limited access express highways for mixed traffic may appropriately be estimated, for purposes of adequacy of design, to have a practical capacity of 1200 to 1500 vehicles per lane per hour. 3.____

4. A city that is growing by constant decennial increments of total population would have a *straight-line* population curve when plotted on semi-logarithmic cross-section paper. 4.____

5. An infant mortality rate of 60 per 1000 live births per annum is representative of good health conditions in northeastern cities of the U.S. 5.____

6. A city which has 4 acres of land in use by industry, per 100 total resident population, would be considered highly industrialized. 6.____

7. The federal government, through the Department of Transportation, assists in financing new state highways within and outside corporate limits of cities. 7.____

8. The "riding habit" of Los Angeles would be expected to be *greater than* that of New York because of greater relative extent of use of private automobiles. 8.____

9. Because of lane friction and traffic weaving, a 4-lane one-way express roadway will NOT achieve a greater vehicle discharge per hour than a 3-lane one-way express roadway, all other design features being the same. 9.____

10. It is *good* practice to locate future playgrounds NOT more than one-quarter mile from any part of residential areas to be served. 10.____

11. An efficiently laid-out 18-hole golf course, under average topographic conditions, can be accomodated within 110 acres. 11.____

12. Elementary school sites of at least 5 acres are representative of good practice. 12.____

13. Senior high school sites of 25 to 40 acres are NOT considered extravagant or excessive under modern design standards. 13.____

14. Future school enrollments can be estimated by extrapolation of a curve showing percentage of total population which was enrolled in the school system in past years. 14.____

15. A "neighborhood unit" is a term used to embrace those planned residential area which constitute area of service of 1 junior high school. 15.____

16. "Company housing" is customarily used to describe colonies of dwelling units owned by an industrial corporation and rented individually to its employees. 16.____

17. In a *well-designed* residential subdivision, area of land in streets should NOT exceed 20 per cent of total area. 17.____

18. It is accepted *good* zoning practice to require large parking areas be screened from adjacent residential zones by landscaping. 18.____

19. "Floor area ratio" is quotient of ground floor area of a building divided by area of its lot. 19.____

20. The term "Unrestricted Districts" designates districts for which no use or area regulations or restrictions are provided by present zoning resolutions. 20.____

21. A rectangular block 200' x 810' has an area of about four acres. 21.____

22. Capacity of a highway *increases* directly with the speed. 22.____

23. A truck farm is prohibited in a residential district. 23.____

24. On a street with a crowned pavement, grade may be reduced to 0.0%. 24.____

25. Climate has NO effect on design of combined sewers. 25.____

26. Subgrade of a highway is the *lowest* grade ensuring adequate drainage. 26.____

27. Underdrainage results when inadequate storm sewers are provided. 27.____

28. Plans for bridges over navigable waterways require Army Corps of Engineers approval. 28.____

29. On a street with crossings at grade, the ONLY safety features added by widening a narrow median strip are further separation of opposing lanes of traffic and reduction of headlight glare. 29.____

30. In rural areas, need of sidewalks along highways depends on density of vehicular and pedestrian traffic and design speed of highway. 30.____

31. It is standard practice to design 2-lane highways with minimum sight distance such that overtaking and passing is possible in any section of the highway. 31.____

32. Widening pavements on curves is for *psychological* reasons ONLY. 32.____

33. An advantage of a concrete pavement is its high salvage value. 33.____

34. A *large* part of city planning consists of correction of mistakes. 34.____

35. Distribution of population is *usually* shown on a dot or density map. 35.____

36. A series of density maps showing population distribution at various dates is of NO more value to a city planner than the latest map of series. 36.____

37. In a *free* port, goods may be stored, repacked, manufactured, and reexported WITHOUT customs formalities. 37.____

38. Urban blight is due *solely* to lack of planning in original development. 38.____

39. The Chamber of Commerce of the United States recommends municipalities adopt building codes permitting use of any material or method of construction which meets minimum required standards of performance.

40. An accepted reliable method of estimating future population of small municipalities (under 10,000), for 5 years forward from the last census, involves extending past trend of birth rates, death rates, annual statistics of new dwelling units constructed, old dwelling units demolished, and average size of family.

KEY (CORRECT ANSWERS)

1.	F	11.	T	21.	T	31.	F
2.	T	12.	T	22.	F	32.	F
3.	T	13.	T	23.	F	33.	T
4.	F	14.	F	24.	F	34.	T
5.	F	15.	F	25.	F	35.	T
6.	T	16.	T	26.	F	36.	F
7.	T	17.	T	27.	F	37.	T
8.	F	18.	T	28.	T	38.	F
9.	F	19.	F	29.	F	39.	T
10.	T	20.	F	30.	T	40.	T

GRAPHS, MAPS, SKETCHES

EXAMINATION SECTION
TEST 1

DIRECTIONS: Each question or incomplete statement is followed by several suggested answers or completions. Select the one that BEST answers the question or completes the statement. *PRINT THE LETTER OF THE CORRECT ANSWER IN THE SPACE AT THE RIGHT.*

Questions 1-7.

DIRECTIONS: Questions 1 to 7, inclusive, are based on information contained on Chart A.

1. Puerto Ricans were the LARGEST number of people in 1.____

   A. 1975   B. 1973   C. 1979   D. 1971

2. At some time between 1974 and 1975, two groups had the same number of persons. These two groups were 2.____

   A. Puerto Rican and Black
   B. Caucasian and Black
   C. Oriental and Black
   D. Puerto Rican and Caucasian

3. In the same year that the Black population reached its GREATEST peak, the LOWEST number of people residing in Revere were of the following group or groups: 3.____

   A. Puerto Rican and Caucasian
   B. Oriental
   C. Puerto Rican
   D. Puerto Rican and Oriental

4. The group which showed the GREATEST increase in population from 1970 to 1979 is 4.____

   A. Puerto Rican
   B. Caucasian
   C. Oriental
   D. not determinable from the graph

5. In 1977, the Black population was higher by APPROXIMATELY 20% over 5.____

   A. 1972   B. 1976   C. 1974   D. 1978

6. The SMALLEST number of people in 1973 were 6.____

   A. Puerto Rican and Black
   B. Oriental and Black
   C. Puerto Rican and Caucasian
   D. Puerto Rican and Oriental

2 (#1)

7. The percent increase in population of Puerto Ricans from 1971 to 1978 is *most nearly*   7.___
   A. 34%   B. 18%   C. 62%   D. 80%

CHART A

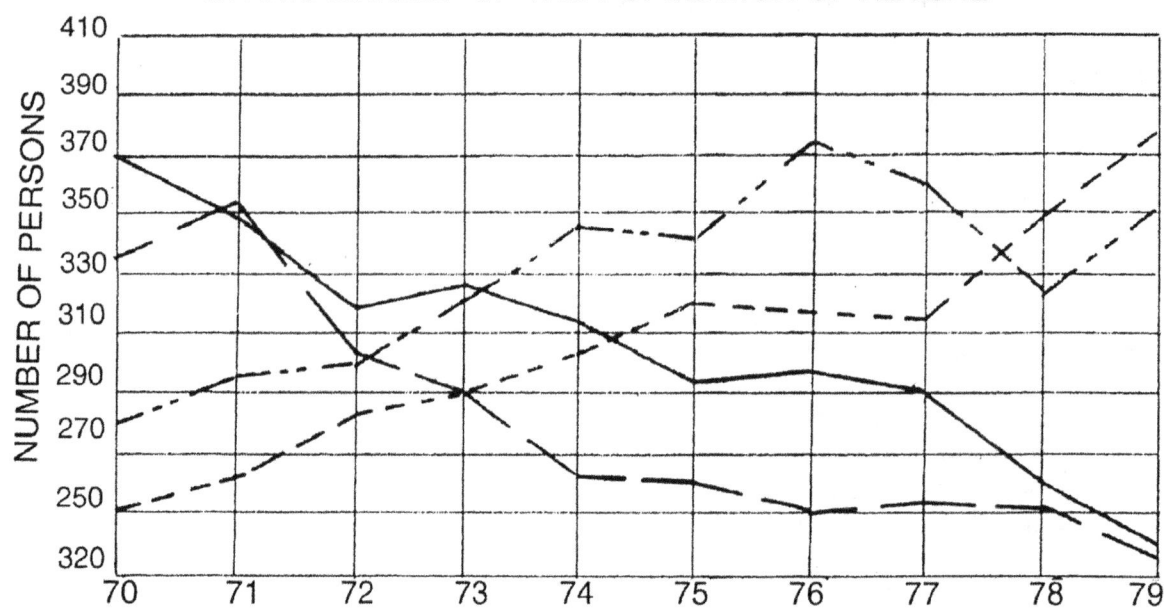

ETHNIC MAKEUP OF THE POPULATION OF REVERE

PUERTO RICAN ----
CAUCASIAN ———
ORIENTAL — —
BLACK — .. —

KEY (CORRECT ANSWERS)

1. C
2. D
3. B
4. A
5. A
6. D
7. A

TEST 2

DIRECTIONS: Each question or incomplete statement is followed by several suggested answers or completions. Select the one that BEST answers the question or completes the statement. *PRINT THE LETTER OF THE CORRECT ANSWER IN THE SPACE AT THE RIGHT.*

Questions 1-2.

DIRECTIONS: Questions 1 and 2 are based on information contained on Chart B.

1. The percent of Black middle students attending overcrowded schools in the period 1967 to 1968 is *most nearly*

    A. 34.6 B. 37.6 C. 44.0 D. 47.5

    1.____

2. The percent growth in total school enrollment between 1960-61 and 1967-68 is *most nearly*

    A. 37.6
    B. 45.7
    C. 35.8
    D. cannot be determined from data given

    2.____

CHART B

Summary: School Utilization and Enrollment

PRIMARY SCHOOLS	1960-61	1967-68
NUMBER OF / PERCENT SCHOOLS / UTILIZATION	20/105	20/102
ENROLLMENT/CAPACITY	16685/15842	18204/17813
UTILIZATION: OVER/UNDER	NET +1942/-1099	NET +2045/-1654
	NO. +843 %	NO. +391 %
WHITE ENROLLMENT	3645 21.8	3146 17.2
NEGRO ENROLLMENT	12691 76.1	14304 78.5
PUERTO RICAN ENROLLMENT	349 2.1	754 4.1

MIDDLE SCHOOLS	1960-61	1967-68
NUMBER OF / PERCENT SCHOOLS / UTILIZATION	3/101	5/96
ENROLLMENT/CAPACITY	4859/4808	7502/7811
UTILIZATION: OVER/UNDER	NET +235/-174	NET +276/-585
	NO. +61 %	NO. -309 %
WHITE ENROLLMENT	1478 30.4	1717 22.8
NEGRO ENROLLMENT	3279 67.3	5228 69.6
PUERTO RICAN ENROLLMENT	112 2.3	557 7.4

HIGH SCHOOLS	1960-61	1967-68
NUMBER OF / PERCENT SCHOOLS / UTILIZATION	2/78	3/107
ENROLLMENT/CAPACITY	1791/2300	6003/5847
UTILIZATION: OVER/UNDER	NET +15/-24	NET +985/-829
	NO. -509 %	NO. +156 %
WHITE ENROLLMENT	1106 61.8	3266 54.4
NEGRO ENROLLMENT	650 36.3	2561 42.6
PUERTO RICAN ENROLLMENT	35 2.0	176 2.9

Detail: School Utilization and Enrollment 1967-1968

PRIMARY SCHOOLS	CONSTRUCTION— DATES AND TYPE*	GRADES	AVERAGE YRS OVER OR UNDER GRADE	SPECIAL PROGRAMS	ENROLLMENT TOTAL	WHITE NO	WHITE %	NEGRO NO	NEGRO %	PUERTO RICAN NO	PUERTO RICAN %	CAPACITY TOTAL	AVAIL- SHORT+	% UTIL	# OF OTHER UTIL ROOMS	
PS 15	1939	K-6	-.1	T,AS	565	34	6.0	523	92.5	40	7.0	669	- 104	84.4		
PS 3C	1965	K-6	+1.2	T,AS	1605	854	53.2	748	46.6	3	.1	1099	+ 506	146.0	18	(NOTE M)
PS 35	1931	K-6	+.6	AS	640	345	53.9	259	40.4	36	5.6	702	- 62	91.1	6	PORTABLES
PS 36	1924,63	K-6	+.3	SS	703	9	1.2	684	97.2	10	1.4	509	+ 194	138.1	6	PORTABLES
PS 37	1928	K-6	+.7	MES,AS	615	61	9.9	544	88.4	10	1.6	419	+ 196	146.7		
PS 40	1912,42,64	K-6	+.8	SS,MES	1058	7	.8	994	93.9	55	5.1	869	+ 189	121.7	6	(NOTE N)
PS 45	1914+28+63	K-6	+.6	SP	986	7	.8	949	96.2	30	3.0	856	+ 130	115.1	4	PORTABLES
PS 48	1936	K-6	+1.2	SS	495	10	2.0	482	97.3	3	.6	632	- 137	78.3	1	(NOTE O)
PS 50	1922	K-6	+.5	SS	772	116	15.0	593	76.8	63	8.1	833	- 61	92.6		
PS 80	1964	K-6	-.1	T,AS	1052	421	40.0	574	54.5	57	5.4	1197	- 145	87.8		
PS 82	1906	K-6	-.3		440	375	85.2	21	4.7	44	10.0	378	+ 62	116.4	2	(NOTE P)
PS 95	1915,25	K-6	-.3	SS	1274	489	38.3	647	50.7	138	10.8	1320	- 46	96.5		
PS 116	1925,64	K-6	-.1	SS	914	2	.2	902	98.6	10	1.0	1067	- 153	85.6		
PS 118	1923,32	K-6	+.0	T	887	28	3.1	832	93.7	27	3.0	1089	- 202	81.4		
PS 123	1928,32,64	K-6	-1.2	SS	1565	41	2.6	1448	92.5	76	4.8	1103	+ 462	141.8	17	PORTABLES
PS 134	1928,38	K-6	-.3	T	1067	42	3.9	959	89.8	66	6.1	761	+ 306	140.2		
PS 136	1928,37	K-6	-.8	T	987	10	1.0	950	96.2	27	2.7	1301	- 314	75.8	1	(NOTE Q)
PS 140	1929,38,63	K-6	-.6	SS	1160	46	3.9	1098	94.6	16	1.3	1241	- 81	93.4		
PS 160	1939	K-6	-.6	SS	1019	11	1.0	1006	98.7	2	.1	1030	- 11	98.9		
PS 178	1951	K-6	+1.8	SS	400	268	67.0	91	22.7	41	10.2	738	- 338	54.2		
TOTAL PRIMARY SCHOOLS=	20				18204	3146	17.2	14304	78.5	754	4.1	17813	+2045 / -1654	102.1		

MIDDLE SCHOOLS																
IS 8	1963	6-8	-.5	SS,PI	1562	325	20.8	1124	71.9	113	7.2	1523	+ 39	102.5		
IS 59	1956	6-8	+.1		1633	621	38.0	846	51.8	166	10.1	1396	+ 237	116.9		
IS 72	1967	6-7	*	PI,T,AS	1396	210	15.0	1171	83.8	15	1.0	1345	+ 251	82.7		
IS 142	1930,38	6-8	-1.5	SS	1096	21	1.9	1004	91.6	71	6.5	1335	- 231	82.1		
JS 192	1963	7-8	-.8		1815	540	29.7	1083	59.6	192	10.5	1912	- 97	94.9		
TOTAL MIDDLE SCHOOLS=	5				7502	1717	22.8	5228	69.6	557	7.4	7811	+ 276 / - 585	96.0		

HIGH SCHOOLS																
SPRINGFELD GDNS	1965	9-12	-.3		4277	2758	64.4	1462	34.1	57	1.3	3292	+ 985	129.9		
JAMAICA VOC	1896—C	9-12	-2.9		644	382	59.3	235	36.4	27	4.1	895	- 251	71.9		
W WILSON VOC	1942	9-12	-3.7		1082	126	11.6	864	79.8	92	8.5	1660	- 578	65.1		
TOTAL HIGH SCHOOLS=	3				6003	3266	54.4	2561	42.6	176	2.9	5847	+ 985 / - 829	102.6		

NOTES
1 INCLUDES ENROLLMENT AND CAPACITY AT ANNEX (PS 170) IN QUEENS PLANNING DISTRICT 8
* EXCEPT AS NOTED ALL SCHOOLS ARE OF FIREPROOF CONSTRUCTION
C NOT FIREPROOF
X NOT AVAILABLE

CODE
T: TRANSITIONAL SCHOOL
AS: AFTER SCHOOL STUDY CENTER
SS: SPECIAL SERVICE SCHOOL
MES: MORE EFFECTIVE SCHOOL
SP: SPECIAL PRIMARY SCHOOL
PI: PILOT INTERMEDIATE SCHOOL

NOTES
M 1M ROCHDALE VILLAGE
N 1 PORTABLE, 2 IM UNION METHODIST CHURCH
O 1M BROOKS MEMORIAL METHODIST CHURCH
P AT 139-35 88TH STREET
Q 1M GRACE METHODIST EPISCOPAL CHURCH

KEY (CORRECT ANSWERS)

1. B
2. C

TEST 3

DIRECTIONS: Each question or incomplete statement is followed by several suggested answers or completions. Select the one that BEST answers the question or completes the statement. *PRINT THE LETTER OF THE CORRECT ANSWER IN THE SPACE AT THE RIGHT.*

Questions 1-4.

DIRECTIONS: Questions 1 to 4, inclusive, are based on the information contained on Chart C.

1. What percent of all households in 1960 are Puerto Rican households with incomes of $6,000 or more per year?

    A. 38%   B. 57%   C. 6%   D. 0.6%

2. The median income in all households in 1960 is in the range of

    A. $3,000 - $5,999
    B. $6,000 - $9,999
    C. $10,000 - $14,999
    D. cannot be determined from data given

3. The total number of white persons living in one or two person households in 1960 is

    A. 13,126   B. 28,884   C. 24,704   D. 46.5

4. Which of the following statements is MOST likely to be true?

    A. In 1970, the majority of the population in the above data is white.
    B. The majority of households in 1960 have incomes under $6,000.
    C. There are 8668 people in 1960 in households with incomes under $3,000.
    D. The majority of households in 1960 with incomes under $2,000 are white.

2 (#3)

CHART C

Population and Housing Data

Housing Units

	TOTAL	1 ROOM	2 ROOMS	3 ROOMS	4 ROOMS	5 ROOMS	6+ ROOMS
TOTAL HOUSING UNITS - 1960	57611	1484	2492	10491	9074	8409	25661
TOTAL OCCUPIED HOUSING UNITS	56107						
RENTER OCCUPIED - TOTAL	23040						
PUBLIC	1048	--	--	44	240	553	199
PUBLICLY AIDED	--	--	--	--	--	--	12
OWNER OCCUPIED - TOTAL	33147						
PUBLIC	--	--	--	--	--	--	--
PUBLICLY AIDED	--	--	--	--	--	--	--
PUBLIC HOUSING - 1970							
PUBLIC RENTER	1434	--	44	321	736	300	33
PUBLICLY AIDED RENTER	65	--	--	22	26	17	--
PUBLICLY AIDED OWNER	6075	--	3	2770	2214	568	520

Population Growth

(line graph showing population from 1950 to 1970, y-axis 0 to 250,000)

Ethnic Make-up (in percent)

White ○
Black ●
Puerto Rican ✱

(bars for 1950, 1960, 1970)

Households 1960 (in percent)

	% OF ALL HOUSEHOLDS	PERSONS IN HOUSEHOLDS					
		1	2	3	4	5	6+
White	56	14	33	21	17	9	7
Black	43	7	23	20	19	13	18
Puerto Rican	1	4	13	17	18	21	27
All Households	100%	12	23	20	17	12	12

Income 1960

	PERSONS IN HOUSEHOLD						TOTAL NUMBER OF HOUSEHOLDS
	1	2	3	4	5	6+	
WHITE HOUSEHOLDS							
UNDER $ 2000	1652	1153	276	143	122		3346
$ 2000 - $ 2999	459	717	176	67	58		1477
$ 3000 - $ 5999	1472	3018	1688	1290	944		8412
$ 6000 - $ 9999	501	3520	2649	2936	1906		10556
$10000 - $14999	75	1378	1255	1069	1144		4925
$15000 AND OVER	17	476	535	637	680		2345
NEGRO AND OTHER NON-WHITE HOUSEHOLDS							
UNDER $ 2000	464	664	366	303	444		2291
$ 2000 - $ 2999	237	453	315	192	280		1477
$ 3000 - $ 5999	587	2368	1721	1304	2313		8293
$ 6000 - $ 9999	98	1735	1984	1650	2465		7932
$10000 - $14999	13	370	547	679	1370		3029
$15000 AND OVER	--	23	82	116	435		656
PUERTO RICAN HOUSEHOLDS							
UNDER $ 2000	9	7	7	11	11		45
$ 2000 - $ 2999	4	7	2	14	12		32
$ 3000 - $ 5999	10	17	45	26	71		169
$ 6000 - $ 9999	--	42	35	30	112		219
$10000 - $14999	--	8	4	21	53		87
$15000 AND OVER	--	1	--	3	19		26
ALL HOUSEHOLDS							
UNDER $ 2000	2155	1824	649	457	577		5682
$ 2000 - $ 2999	700	1170	493	273	350		2986
$ 3000 - $ 5999	2069	5403	3454	2620	3328		16874
$ 6000 - $ 9999	599	5297	4668	4616	4477		18657
$10000 - $14999	92	1756	1807	1769	2567		8041
$15000 AND OVER	17	499	621	756	1134		3027

KEY (CORRECT ANSWERS)

1. D
2. B
3. C
4. D

———

TEST 4

DIRECTIONS: Each question or incomplete statement is followed by several suggested answers or completions. Select the one that BEST answers the question or completes the statement. *PRINT THE LETTER OF THE CORRECT ANSWER IN THE SPACE AT THE RIGHT.*

Questions 1-4.

DIRECTIONS: Questions 1 through 4, inclusive, are based on information contained on Chart D.

1. The percentage of households by ethnic make-up in 1960 was *most nearly* 1.____

    A. 16% white, 12% Black and other non-white, 16% Puerto Rican, and 56% not reported
    B. 39% white, 26% Black and other non-white, and 35% Puerto Rican
    C. 95% white, 3% Black and 2% Puerto Rican
    D. 99% white, 1% Black and other non-white, and 0% Puerto Rican

2. In 1960, the predominant age group was in the age range of 2.____

    A. 5-15 B. 25-44 C. 45-64 D. 0-15

3. In 1960, the LARGEST singular and discrete income group consisted of households with the following characteristics: 3.____

    A. Black and other non-white households of 3 persons with total earnings of between $6,000 and $9,999
    B. White households with 3 persons with total earnings from under $2,000 to $5,999
    C. White households of 2 persons with total earnings between $6,000 and $9,999
    D. White households with total earnings under $2,000

4. The percent population increase between 1950 and 1970 was most nearly 4.____

    A. 56% B. 30% C. 25% D. 33%

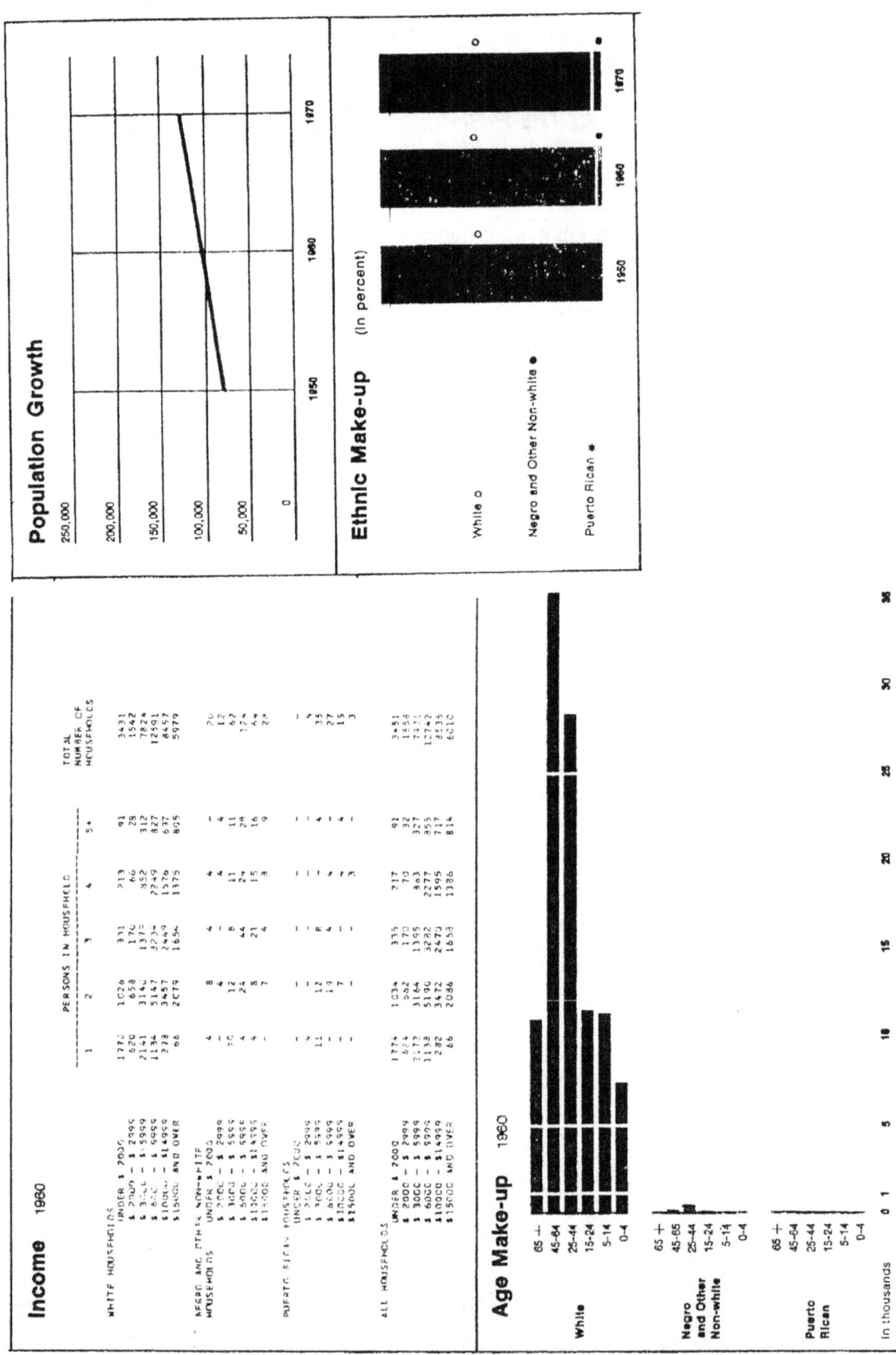

CHART D

KEY (CORRECT ANSWERS)

1. D
2. C
3. C
4. A

TEST 5

DIRECTIONS: Each question or incomplete statement is followed by several suggested answers or completions. Select the one that BEST answers the question or completes the statement. *PRINT THE LETTER OF THE CORRECT ANSWER IN THE SPACE AT THE RIGHT.*

Questions 1-3.

DIRECTIONS: Questions 1 through 3, inclusive, are based on information contained on Zoning Map E. Zoning Map E is drawn to scale. Candidates are to scale off measurements.

1. One-third of Block A (shaded area) has already been developed as a public housing project. It is proposed that a second development be built on the remainder of the site. The approximate size of the proposed site, in acres, is *most nearly* (43,650 sq.ft. = 1 acre)

    A. 5.9   B. 55   C. 1.8   D. 10.3

    1.___

2. If Site B were developed for housing and 40% of the site was covered by buildings, the amount of open space would be *most nearly* _____ acres.

    A. 2.5   B. 6.3   C. 3.8   D. 2.7

    2.___

3. A new elementary school will have to be built to accommodate the children from the two proposed projects at A and B.
   If the new school must be within 1/2 mile walk of any point in either project, which would be the *most likely* site?

    A. 1   B. 2   C. 3   D. 4

    3.___

2 (#5)

ZONING MAP E

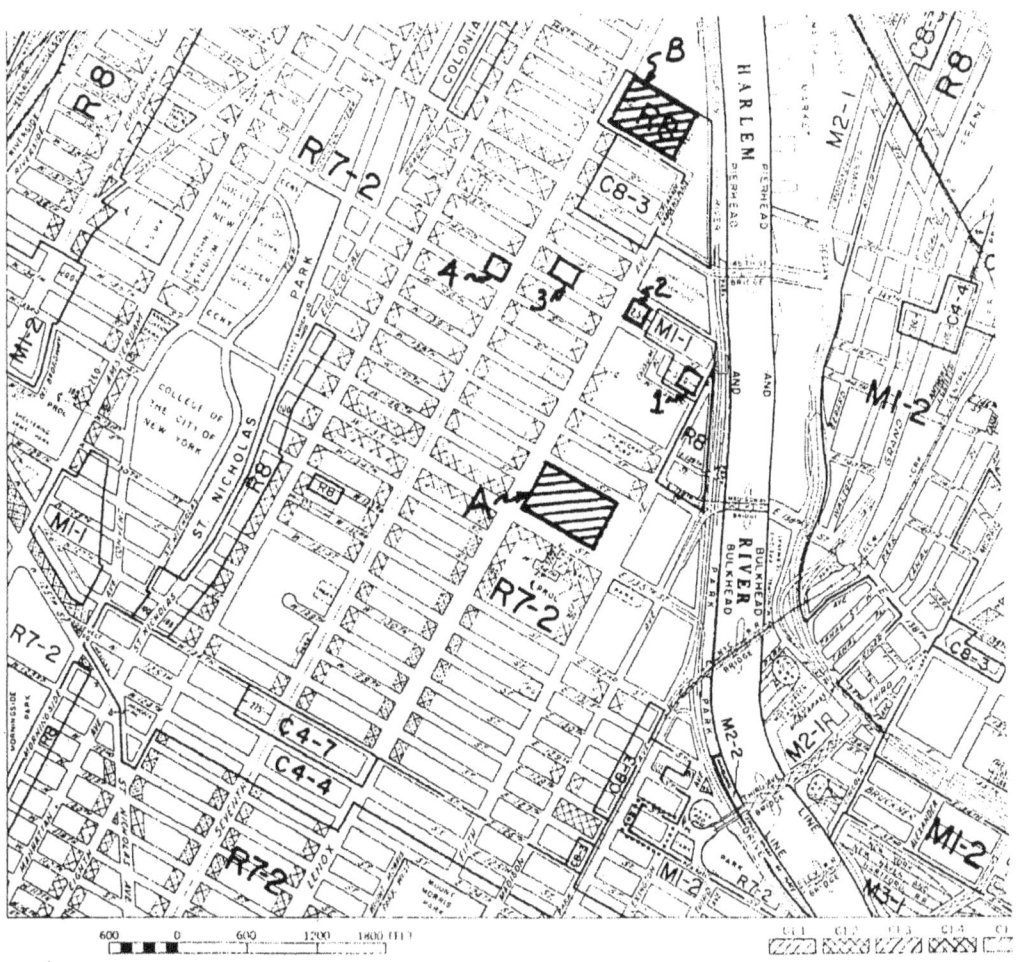

KEY (CORRECT ANSWERS)

1. A
2. C
3. B

TEST 6

DIRECTIONS: Each question or incomplete statement is followed by several suggested answers or completions. Select the one that BEST answers the question or completes the statement. *PRINT THE LETTER OF THE CORRECT ANSWER IN THE SPACE AT THE RIGHT.*

Questions 1-2.

DIRECTIONS: Questions 1 and 2 are to be answered in accordance with the Coast and Geodetic Map F.

1. The difference in elevation between the lowest and highest point of Ewen Park is *most nearly* _____ feet.

   A. 100   B. 25   C. 200   D. 50

   1.____

2. Given: The scale of the map is as shown.
   The distance between the College of Mt. St. Vincent and Ewen Park is *most nearly* _____ feet.

   A. 2,000   B. 6,000   C. 24,000   D. 12,000

   2.____

2 (#6)

COAST & GEODETIC MAP F

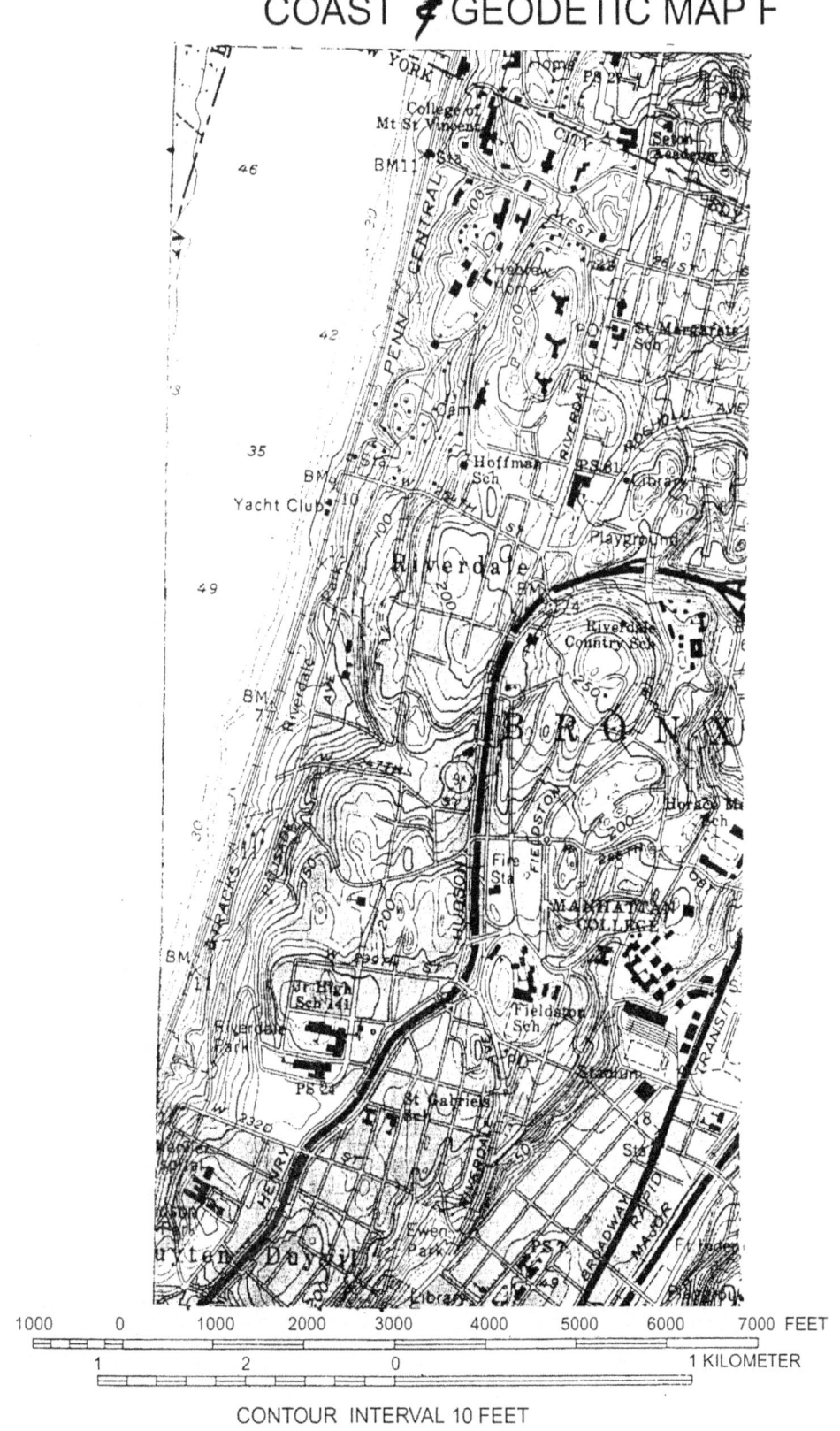

CONTOUR INTERVAL 10 FEET

KEY (CORRECT ANSWERS)

1. A
2. D

TEST 7

DIRECTIONS: Each question or incomplete statement is followed by several suggested answers or completions. Select the one that BEST answers the question or completes the statement. *PRINT THE LETTER OF THE CORRECT ANSWER IN THE SPACE AT THE RIGHT.*

Questions 1-3.

DIRECTIONS: Questions 1 to 3, inclusive, are based on information contained on Sketch G, a birds-eye view of a proposed development.

NOTE: The attached single family homes in the periphery are one-story high and contain 1,000 square feet. They are square buildings.

1. The dimension A of this single family attached home is *most nearly* _____ feet. 1.____
   A. 20   B. 32   C. 50   D. 100

2. The dimension B of the road is *most nearly* _____ feet. 2.____
   A. 25   B. 48   C. 75   D. 100

3. The dimension C of the courtyard is *most nearly* _____ feet. 3.____
   A. 40   B. 85   C. 57   D. 150

2 (#7)

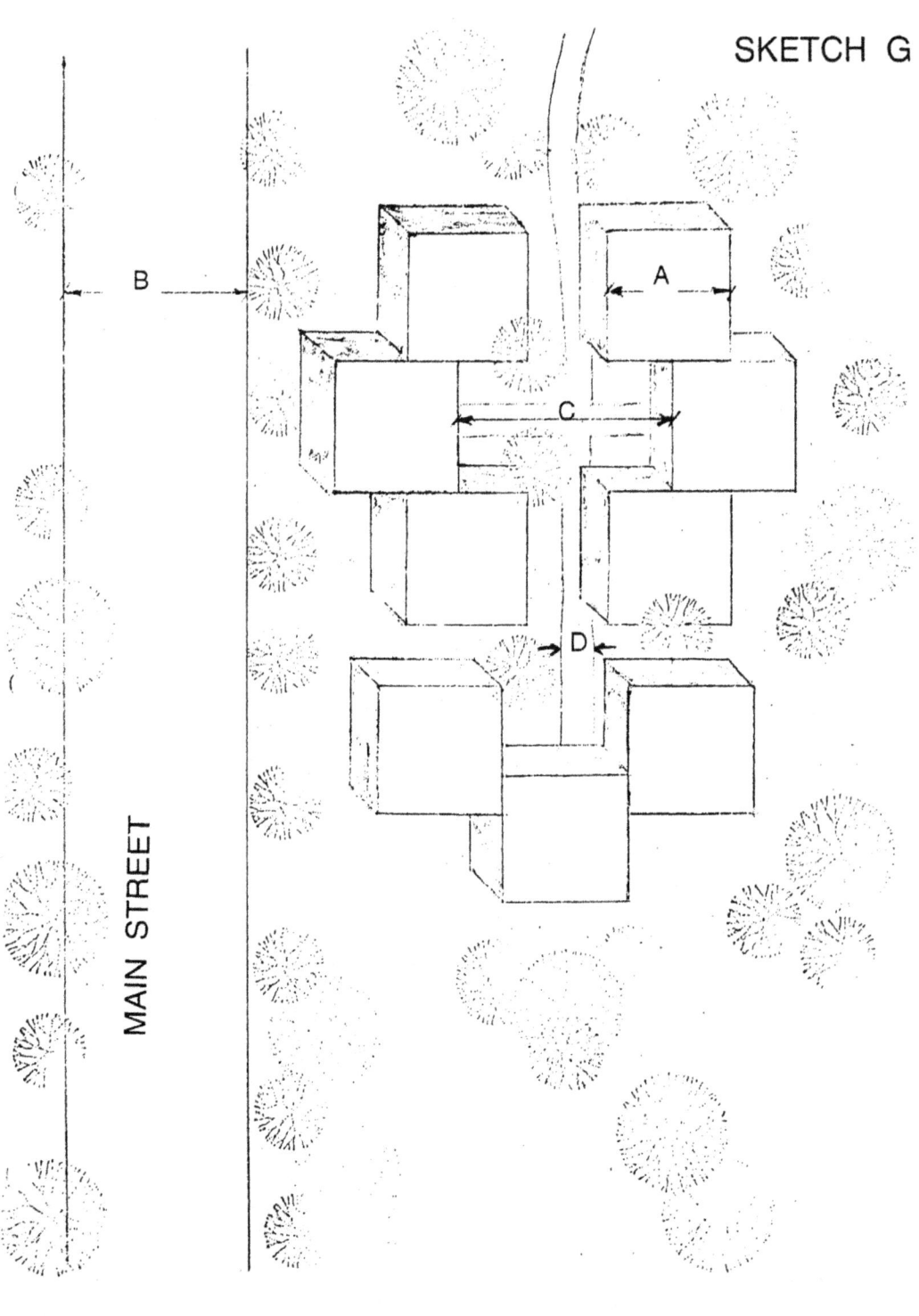

SKETCH G

MAIN STREET

KEY (CORRECT ANSWERS)

1. B
2. B
3. C

INTERPRETING STATISTICAL DATA GRAPHS, CHARTS AND TABLES
EXAMINATION SECTION
TEST 1

DIRECTIONS: Each question or incomplete statement is followed by several suggested answers or completions. Select the one that BEST answers the question or completes the statement. *PRINT THE LETTER OF THE CORRECT ANSWER IN THE SPACE AT THE RIGHT.*

Questions 1-5.

DIRECTIONS: Questions 1 through 5 are to be answered SOLELY on the basis of the information given in the table below.

AGE COMPOSITION IN THE LABOR FORCE IN CITY A (1990-2000)					
	Age Group	1990	1995	2000
Men	14-24	8,430	10,900	14,340
	25-44	22,200	22,350	26,065
	45+	17,550	19,800	21,970
Women	14-24	4,450	6,915	7,680
	25-44	9,080	10,010	11,550
	45+	7,325	9,470	13,180

1. The GREATEST increase in the number of people in the labor force between 1990 and 1995 occurred among

   A. men between the ages of 14 and 24
   B. men age 45 and over
   C. women between the ages of 14 and 24
   D. women age 45 and over

   1._____

2. If the total number of women of all ages in the labor force increases from 2000 to 2005 by the same number as it did from 1995 to 2000, the TOTAL number of women of all ages in the labor force in 2005 will be

   A. 27,425   B. 29,675   C. 37,525   D. 38,425

   2._____

3. The total increase in numbers of women in the labor force from 1990 to 1995 differs from the total increase of men in the same years by being _____ than that of men.

   A. 770 less   B. 670 more
   C. 770 more   D. 1,670 more

   3._____

4. In the year 1990, the proportion of married women in each group was as follows: 1/5 of the women in the 14-24 age group, 1/4 of those in the 25-44 age group, and 2/5 of those 45 and over.
   How many married women were in the labor force in 1990?

   A. 4,625   B. 5,990   C. 6,090   D. 7,910

   4._____

117

5. The 14-24 age group of men in the labor force from 1990 to 2000 increased by APPROXIMATELY

    A. 40%   B. 65%   C. 70%   D. 75%

KEY (CORRECT ANSWERS)

1. A
2. D
3. B
4. C
5. C

TEST 2

Questions 1-5.

DIRECTIONS: Questions 1 through 5 are to be answered SOLELY on the basis of the information given in the table below.

TYPE OF AREA	ACRES PER 1,000 POPULATION	SIZE OF SITE (ACRES)		RADIUS OF AREAS SERVED (MILES)
		IDEAL	MINIMUM	
Playgrounds	1.5	4	2	0.5
Neighborhood parks	2.0	10	5	0.5
Playfields	1.5	15	10	1.5
Community parks	3.5	100	40	2.0
District parks	2.0	200	100	3.0
Regional parks and reservations	15.0	500-1,000	varies	10.0

STANDARDS FOR RECREATION AREAS

1. What is the MINIMUM number of playfields that a community of 15,000 people may contain if the size of each is kept within the limits shown in the table?

   A. 4   B. 10   C. 6   D. 2

2. If, as far as possible, ideal sized playgrounds are built, how many ideal sized playgrounds should a community of 12,000 people contain?

   A. 4   B. 8   C. 1   D. 10

3. APPROXIMATELY how many people can a community park of 200 acres serve?

   A. 120,000   B. 80,000   C. 55,000   D. 20,000

4. If only minimum sized neighborhood parks are built, how many will be required for a population of 20,000?

   A. 5   B. 2   C. 8   D. 12

5. A community of 75,000 persons is evenly distributed over a 5 square mile area. Of the following, the number and size of playgrounds that would BEST satisfy the standards is _____ playgrounds at _____ acres each.

   A. 5;7.5   B. 35;3.5   C. 10;10   D. 50;1.5

KEY (CORRECT ANSWERS)

1. D
2. A
3. C
4. C
5. B

TEST 3

Questions 1-6.

DIRECTIONS: Questions 1 through 6 are to be answered SOLELY on the basis of the following chart.

In a national study of poverty trends, the following data have been assembled for interpretation.

PERSONS BELOW POVERTY LEVEL BY RESIDENCE				
	Number (millions)		Percent	
Item	U.S.	Metropolitan Areas	U.S.	Metropolitan Areas
1999				
Total	38.8	17.0	22.0	15.3
Under 25 years	20.0	8.8	25.3	18.1
65 years	5.5		35.2	26.9
Black	9.9	5.0	55.1	42.8
Other	28.3	11.8	18.1	12.0
2009				
Total	24.3	12.3	12.2	9.5
Under 25 years	12.2		13.2	10.4
65 years & over	4.8	2.3	25.3	20.2
Black	7.2	3.9	32.3	24.4
Other	16.7	8.2	9.5	7.3

1. If no other source of data were available, which of the following groups would you expect to have the HIGHEST rate of poverty?

   A. Others over 65
   B. Others under 65
   C. Blacks over 65
   D. Blacks under 65

2. Between 1999 and 2009, the percentage of poor in the United States who were Black

   A. increased from 25.5% to 29.6%
   B. decreased from 55.1% to 32.3%
   C. decreased from 9.9% to 7.2%
   D. stayed the same

3. The data in the second column of the table indicate that, in metropolitan areas, the number of poor declined by 4.7 million of 36.2% between 1999 and 2009. Yet, the fourth column shows a corresponding decline from 15.3% to 9.5%, or only 5.8%.
   This apparent discrepancy reflects the fact that the

   A. metropolitan areas are growing while the number of poor is contracting
   B. two columns in question are based on different sources of information
   C. difference between two percentages is not the same as the percent change in total numbers
   D. tables have inherent errors and must be carefully checked

4. The percentages in each of the last two columns of the table for 1999 and 2009 don't add up to 100%.
   This is for the reason that

   A. rounding off each entry to the nearest decimal place caused an error in the total such that the total is not equal to 100%
   B. these columns show the percentage of Blacks, aged, etc. who are poor rather than the percentage of poor who are Black, aged, etc.
   C. there was an error in the construction of the table which was not noticed until the table was already in print
   D. there is double counting in the entries in the table; some people are counted more than once

5. Data such as that presented in the table on persons below poverty level are shown to a single decimal place because

   A. data in every table should always be shown to a single decimal place
   B. it is the minimal number of decimal places needed to distinguish among table entries
   C. there was no room for more decimal places in the table without crowding
   D. the more accurately a figure is shown, the better it is for the user

6. In comparing the poverty of the young (under 25 years) with that of the older population (65 years and over) in 1999 and 2009, one could REASONABLY conclude that

   A. more young people than old people were poor but older people had a higher rate of poverty
   B. more older people than young people were poor but young people had a higher rate of poverty
   C. there is a greater degree of poverty among the younger population than among the older people
   D. young people and old people have the same rate of poverty

---

KEY (CORRECT ANSWERS)

1. C
2. B
3. C
4. B
5. D
6. A

TEST 4

Questions 1-5.

DIRECTIONS: Questions 1 through 5 are to be answered SOLELY on the basis of the table shown below.

POPULATION, URBAN AND RURAL, BY RACE: 1980 TO 2000

In thousands, except percent. An urbanized area comprises at least 1 city of 50,000 inhabitants (central city) plus contiguous closely settled areas (urban fringe). Data for 1980 and 1990 according to urban definition used in the 1990 census; 2000 data according to the 2000 definition.

YEAR AND AREA	TOTAL	WHITE	BLACK AND OTHER	% DISTRIBUTION TOTAL	WHITE	BLACK AND OTHER
1980, total population	151,326	135,150	16,176	100.0	100.0	100.0
Urban	96,847	86,864	9,983	64.0	64.3	61.7
Inside urbanized areas	69,249	61,925	7,324	45.8	45.8	45.3
Central cities	48,377	42,042	6,335	32.0	31.1	39.2
Urban fringe	20,872	19,883	989	13.8	14.7	6.1
Outside urbanized areas	27,598	24,939	2,659	18.2	18.5	16.4
Rural	54,479	48,286	6,193	36.0	35.7	38.3
1990, total population	179,323	158,832	20,491	100.0	100.0	100.0
Urban	125,269	110,428	14,840	69.9	69.5	72.4
Inside urbanized areas	95,848	83,770	12,079	53.5	52.7	58.9
Central cities	57,975	47,627	10,348	32.3	30.0	50.5
Urban fringe	37,873	36,143	1,371	21.1	22.8	8.4
Outside urbanized areas	29,420	26,658	2,762	16.4	16.8	13.5
Rural	54,054	48,403	5,651	30.1	30.5	27.6
2000, total population	203,212	177,749	25,463	100.0	100.0	100.0
Urban	149,325	128,773	20,552	73.5	72.4	80.7
Inside urbanized areas	118,447	100,952	17,495	58.3	56.8	68.7
Central cities	63,922	49,547	14,375	31.5	27.9	56.5
Urban fringe	54,525	51,405	3,120	26.8	28.9	12.3
Outside urbanized areas	30,878	27,822	3,057	15.2	15.7	12.0
Rural	53,887	48,976	4,911	26.5	27.6	19.3

1. The ratio of urban to rural population in 1980 was MOST NEARLY

    A. 3:1   B. 4:1   C. 2:1   D. 1 1/2:1

2. According to the table, the trend of population inside urban areas has been

   A. towards greater concentration
   B. towards less concentration
   C. towards stabilization
   D. erratic

3. Since 1980, the urban fringe white population has substantially increased, while the urban fringe Black and other population has

   A. slightly decreased
   B. greatly decreased
   C. remained the same
   D. increased moderately

4. Over the years, the percentage of the urban white population as compared with the percentage of the total urban population has

   A. remained relatively constant
   B. substantially decreased
   C. substantially increased
   D. varied

5. Select the one of the following which BEST describes the central city white population rate of decrease since 1980 as compared with the central city Black population rate of increase.

   A. The central city white population rate of decrease has been GREATER THAN the central city Black population rate of increase.
   B. The central city white and Black populations have NOT INCREASED to a significant degree.
   C. The central city white population rate of decrease has been EQUAL to the central city Black population rate of increase.
   D. The central city white population rate of decrease has been LESS THAN the central city Black population rate of increase.

KEY (CORRECT ANSWERS)

1. C
2. A
3. D
4. A
5. D

TEST 5

Questions 1-5.

DIRECTIONS: Questions 1 through 4 are to be answered SOLELY on the basis of the information given in the table below.

LIVE BIRTHS, DEATHS, MARRIAGES, AND DIVORCES: 1950-2001									
	Number (1,000)					Rate per 1,000 population			
		DEATHS		MAR-	DIVOR		DEATHS		MAR- DIVOR-
YEAR	BIRTHS	TOTAL	INFANT	RIAGES	-CES	BIRTHS	TOTAL	INFANT	RIAGES CES
1950	2,777	697	(NA)	948	83	30.1	14.7	(NA)	10.3 0.9
1955	2,965	816	78	1,008	104	29.5	13.2	99.9	10.0 1.0
1960	2,950	1,118	130	1,274	171	27.7	13.0	85.8	12.0 1.6
1965	2,909	1,192	135	1,188	175	25.1	11.7	71.7	10.3 1.5
1970	2,618	1,327	142	1,127	196	21.3	11.3	64.6	9.2 1.6
1975	2,377	1,393	120	1,327	218	18.7	10.9	55.7	10.4 1.7
1980	2,559	1,417	111	1,596	264	19.4	10.8	47.0	12.1 2.0
1985	2,858	1,402	105	1,613	485	20.4	10.6	38.3	12.2 3.5
1990	3,632	1,452	104	1,667	385	24.1	9.6	29.2	11.1 2.6
1995	4,104	1,529	107	1,531	377	25.0	9.3	26.4	9.3 2.3
2000	4,258	1,712	111	1,523	393	23.7	9.5	26.0	8.5 2.2
2001	4,268	1,702	108	1,548	414	23.3	9.3	25.3	8.5 2.3

NA - Not available

1. From 1950 to 2001, the birth rate

   A. approximately doubled
   B. remained stable
   C. been reduced by 25%
   D. had two breaks in its downward progression

2. A comparison of the total population death rate to the infant death rate shows that

   A. the two rates have remained constant
   B. the infant death rate is greater
   C. the total population death rate has decreased at a faster rate
   D. infants had a greater chance to survive in 1955 than in 1990

3. In 1955, about one marriage out of ten ended in divorce.
   In which of the following years would the rate be LESS?

   A. 1995   B. 1975   C. 1960   D. 1950

4. The significance of the decrease in the infant death rate is that 4.____
   A. family size will increase
   B. family size will decrease
   C. family size will not be affected
   D. children will become a smaller percentage of the total population

KEY (CORRECT ANSWERS)

1. C
2. B
3. D
4. C

TEST 6

Questions 1-3.

DIRECTIONS: Questions 1 through 3 are to be answered SOLELY on the basis of the information given in the table below.

The age characteristics of the total population in a certain neighborhood are as follows:

AGE	NUMBER OF PEOPLE
3	2
5	4
12	3
18	3
20	1
21	3
22	4
50	2
56	1
72	2

5. The mean age of the population in the neighborhood described above is MOST NEARLY 5.___

   A. 15   B. 19   C. 23   D. 27

6. The median age of the population in the neighborhood described above is MOST NEARLY 6.___

   A. 15   B. 20   C. 25   D. 30

7. The percentage of the population over age 65 in the neighborhood described above is MOST NEARLY 7.___

   A. 2   B. 4   C. 6   D. 8

KEY (CORRECT ANSWERS)

1. C
2. B
3. D

READING COMPREHENSION
UNDERSTANDING AND INTERPRETING WRITTEN MATERIAL

EXAMINATION SECTION

DIRECTIONS: Each question or incomplete statement is followed by several suggested answers or completions. Select the one that BEST answers the question or completes the statement. *PRINT THE LETTER OF THE CORRECT ANSWER IN THE SPACE AT THE RIGHT.*

TEST 1

Questions 1-2.

DIRECTIONS: Questions 1 and 2 are to be answered SOLELY on the basis of the following passage.

One of the biggest mistakes of government executives with substantial supervisory responsibility is failing to make careful appraisals of performance during employee probationary periods. Many a later headache could have been avoided by prompt and full appraisal during the early months of an employee's assignment. There is not much more to say about this except to emphasize the common prevalence of this oversight and to underscore that for its consequences, which are many and sad, the offending managers have no one to blame but themselves.

1. According to the above passage, probationary periods are
    A. a mistake and should not be used by supervisors with large responsibilities
    B. not used properly by government executives
    C. used only for those with supervisory responsibility
    D. the consequence of management mistakes

2. The one of the following conclusions that can MOST appropriately be drawn from the above passage is that
    A. management's failure to appraise employees during their probationary period is a common occurrence
    B. there is not much to say about probationary periods because they are unimportant
    C. managers should blame employees for failing to use their probationary periods properly
    D. probationary periods are a headache to most managers

Questions 3-7.

DIRECTIONS: Questions 3 through 7 are to be answered SOLELY on the basis of the passage preceding each question.

3. Things may not always be what they seem to be. Thus, the wise supervisor should analyze his problems and determine whether there is something there that does not meet the eye. For example, what may seem on the surface to be a personality clash between two subordinates may really be a problem of faulty organization, bad communication, or bad scheduling.
Which one of the following statements BEST supports this passage?
   A. The wise supervisor should avoid personality clashes.
   B. The smart supervisor should figure out what really is going on.
   C. Bad scheduling is the result of faulty organization.
   D. The best supervisor is the one who communicates effectively.

4. Some supervisors, under the pressure of meeting deadlines, become harsh and dictatorial to their subordinates. However, the supervisor most likely to be effective in meeting deadlines is one who absorbs or cushions pressures from above. According to the above passage, if a supervisor wishes to meet deadlines, it is MOST important that he
   A. be informative to his superiors
   B. encourage personal initiative among his subordinates
   C. become harsh and dictatorial to his subordinates
   D. protects his subordinates from pressures from above

5. When giving instructions, a supervisor must always make clear his meaning, leaving no room for misunderstanding. For example, a supervisor who tells a subordinate to do a task *as soon as possible* might legitimately be understood to mean either *it's top priority* or *do it when you can*. Which of the following statements is BEST supported by the above passage?
   A. Subordinates will attempt to avoid work by deliberately distorting instructions.
   B. Instructions should be short, since brief instructions are the clearest.
   C. Less educated subordinates are more likely to honestly misunderstand instructions.
   D. A supervisor should give precise instructions that cannot be misinterpreted.

6. Practical formulas are often suggested to simplify what a supervisor should know and how he should behave, such as the four F's (be firm, fair, friendly, and factual). But such simple formulas are really broad principles, not necessarily specific guides in a real situation. According to the above passage, simple formulas for supervisory behavior
   A. are superior to complicated theories and principles
   B. not always of practical use in actual situations
   C. useful only if they are fair and factual
   D. would be better understood if written in clear language

7. Many management decisions are made far removed from the actual place of operations. Therefore, there is a great need for reliable reports and records and, the larger the organization, the greater is the need for such reports and records. According to the above passage, management decisions made far from the place of operations are
   A. dependent to a great extent on reliable reports and records
   B. sometimes in error because of the great distances involved
   C. generally unreliable because of poor communications
   D. generally more accurate than on-the-scene decisions

Questions 8-9.

DIRECTIONS: Questions 8 and 9 are to be answered SOLELY on the basis of the following passage.

A supervisor who is seeking to influence the behavior of others, whether these others are subordinates, superiors, or colleagues, soon becomes aware of the importance of their attitudes. He may be surprised at some of the attitudes they have and wonder how they can hold some of the views they do - if these views differ from his own. He may be perplexed when others do not change their attitudes even after he has presented facts that obviously should cause them to change.

8. Of the following, the MAIN implication of the above passage is that   8._____
   A. behavior is influenced by factual data
   B. interaction with others is based on factual data
   C. rank and intelligence determine behavior
   D. interpretation of facts is controlled by attitude

9. The one of the following statements MOST directly supported by the above paragraph is: 9._____
   A. A competent supervisor is firm in his views yet retains an open mind
   B. Influencing the behavior of others is usually the most difficult problem in effective supervision
   C. A particular viewpoint may seem unusual to a supervisor holding a contrary opinion
   D. Organizational success depends upon supervisory motivation

Questions 10-13.

DIRECTIONS: Questions 10 through 13 are to be answered SOLELY on the basis of the following passage.

Top public officials, who feel they have tried to improve conditions for their employees, are often bewildered, hurt, or angered when these employees want to do something on their own through union membership. These officials gain little, however, by regarding unionization as an insult or as evidence of failure on their part. The real challenge and opportunity for top officials is to deal constructively with the labor organization which their employees have *duly* chosen to represent them.

10. The author of the above passage MOST likely considers top management to be   10._____
    A. corrupt   B. independent
    C. entrenched   D. paternalistic

11. The above passage points out that certain top public officials are LIKELY to be   11._____
    A. disturbed that employees wish to be unionized
    B. aware of the actual needs of their employees
    C. convinced that labor organizations are ineffectual in gaining benefits
    D. unable to deal constructively with individual employees

12. The tenor of the above passage suggests that
    A. top officials should deal positively with the labor organization
    B. intelligent management practices usually eliminate labor union activities
    C. the labor movement has often opposed enlightened management policies
    D. labor and management have had a long history of disagreement

13. As used in the above passage, the word *duly* means MOST NEARLY
    A. properly or legally
    B. forcefully or sincerely
    C. openly or publicly
    D. precisely or carefully

Questions 14-17.

DIRECTIONS: Questions 14 through 17 are to be answered SOLELY on the basis of the following passage.

The mental attitude of the employee toward safety is exceedingly important in preventing accidents. All efforts designed to keep safety on the employee's mind and to keep accident prevention a live subject in the office will help substantially in a safety program. Although it may seem strange, it is common for people to be careless. Therefore, safety education is a continuous process.

Safety rules should be explained, and the reasons for their rigid enforcement should be given to employees. Telling employees to be careful or giving similar general safety warnings and slogans is probably of little value. Employees should be informed of basic safety fundamentals. This can be done through staff meetings, informal suggestions to employees, movies, and safety instruction cards. Safety instruction cards provide the employees with specific suggestions about safety and serve as a series of timely reminders helping to keep safety on the minds of employees. Pictures, posters, and cartoon sketches on bulletin boards that are located in areas continually used by employees arouse the employees' interest in safety. It is usually good to supplement this type of safety promotion with intensive individual follow-up.

14. The above passage implies that the LEAST effective of the following safety measures is
    A. rigid enforcement of safety rules
    B. getting employees to think in terms of safety
    C. elimination of unsafe conditions in the office
    D. telling employees to stay alert at all times

15. The reason given by the above passage for maintaining ongoing safety education is that
    A. people are often careless
    B. office tasks are often dangerous
    C. the value of safety slogans increases with repetition
    D. safety rules change frequently

16. Which one of the following safety aids is MOST likely to be preferred by the above passage?
    A
    A. cartoon of a man tripping over a carton and yelling, *Keep aisles clear!*
    B. poster with a large number one and a caption saying, *Safety First*
    C. photograph of a very neatly arranged office
    D. large sign with the word *THINK* in capital letters

17. Of the following, the BEST title for the above passage is
    A. BASIC SAFETY FUNDAMENTALS
    B. ENFORCING SAFETY AMONG CARELESS EMPLOYEES
    C. ATTITUDES TOWARD SAFETY
    D. MAKING EMPLOYEES AWARE OF SAFETY

Questions 18-21.

DIRECTIONS: Questions 18 through 21 are to be answered SOLELY on the basis of the following passage.

An employee who has been a member of the retirement system continuously for at least two years may thereafter borrow an amount not exceeding forty percent of the amount of his accumulated contributions in the retirement system, provided that he can repay the amount borrowed, with interest, before he reaches age sixty-three by additional deductions of eight percent from his compensation at the time it is paid. The rate of interest payable on such loan shall be three percent higher than the rate of regular interest creditable to his retirement account. The amount borrowed, with interest, shall be repaid in equal installments by deduction from the member's compensation at the time it is paid, but such installments must be equal to at least four percent of the member's compensation.

Each loan shall be insured by the retirement system against the death of the member, as follows: from the twenty-fifth through the fiftieth day after making the loan, thirty percent of the present value of the loan is insured; from the fifty-first through the seventy-fifth day, sixty percent of the present value of the loan is insured; on and after the seventy-sixth day, all of the present value of the loan is insured. Upon the death of the member, the amount of insurance payable shall be credited to his accumulated contributions to the retirement system.

Instead of a loan, any member who cancels his rate of contribution may withdraw from his account, and may restore in any year he chooses, any sum in excess of the maximum in his annuity savings account and due to his account at the end of the calendar year in which he was entitled to cancel his rate of contribution.

18. Based on the information in the above passage, a member may obtain a loan
    A. in any amount not exceeding forty percent of his accumulated contributions in the system
    B. if he has contributions in excess of the maximum in his annuity savings account
    C. if he will remain a member of the retirement system until age 63
    D. once during his first two years of membership and then at any time thereafter

19. According to the information in the above passage, the interest rate paid by a member who borrows from the retirement system is
    A. 4% of his earnable compensation
    B. 8% of his earnable compensation
    C. lower than the interest rate creditable to his retirement account
    D. higher than the interest rate creditable to his retirement account

19.____

20. Suppose that a member of the retirement system obtained a loan on July 15 of this year and died on October 2 when the present value of her loan was $800. Based on the information in the above passage, this member will have _____ her accumulated contributions to the retirement system.
    A. $480 credited to   B. $480 deducted from
    C. $800 credited to   D. $800 deducted from

20.____

21. Based on the information in the above passage, a member who has excess funds in his retirement account may with- draw funds from the retirement system
    A. if he has cancelled his rate of contribution
    B. if he restores the funds within one year of withdrawal
    C. when he retires
    D. if he leaves city service

21.____

Questions 22-25.

DIRECTIONS: Questions 22 through 25 are to be answered SOLELY on the basis of the following passage.

Upon the death of a member or former member of the retirement system, there shall be paid to his estate, or to the person he had nominated by written designation, his accumulated deductions. In addition, if he is a member who is in city service, there shall be paid a sum consisting of: an amount equal to the compensation he earned while a member during the three months immediately preceding his death, or, if the total amount of years of allowable service exceeds five, there shall be paid an amount equal to the compensation he earned while a member during the six months immediately preceding his death; and the reserve-for-increased-take-home-pay, if any. Payment for the expense of burial, not exceeding two hundred and fifty dollars, may be made to the relative or friend who, in the absence or failure of the designated beneficiary, assumes this responsibility.

Until the first retirement benefit payment has been made, where a member has not selected an option, the member will be considered to be in city service, and the death benefits provided above will be paid instead of the retirement allowance. The member, or upon his death his designated beneficiary, may provide that the actuarial equivalent of the benefit otherwise payable in a lump sum shall be paid in the form of an annuity payable in installments; the amount of such annuity is determined at the time of the member's death on the basis of the age of the beneficiary at that time.

7 (#1)

22. Suppose that a member who has applied for retirement benefits without selecting an option dies before receiving any payments.
According to the information in the above passage, this member's beneficiary would be entitled to receive
    A. an annuity based on the member's age at the time of his death
    B. a death benefit only
    C. the member's retirement allowance only
    D. the member's retirement allowance, plus a death benefit payment in a lump sum

22._____

23. According to the information in the above passage, the amount of the benefit payable upon the death of a member is based, in part, on the
    A. length of city service during which the deceased person was a member
    B. number of beneficiaries the deceased member had nominated
    C. percent of the deceased member's deductions for social security
    D. type of retirement plan to which the deceased member belonged

23._____

24. According to the information in the above passage, which one of the following statements concerning the payment of death benefits is CORRECT?
    A. In order for a death benefit to be paid, the deceased member must have previously nominated, in writing, someone to receive the benefit.
    B. Death benefits are paid upon the death of members who are in city service.
    C. A death benefit must be paid in one lump sum.
    D. When a retired person dies, his retirement allowance is replaced by a death benefit payment.

24._____

25. According to the information in the above passage, the amount of annuity payments made to a beneficiary in monthly installments in lieu of a lump sum payment is determined by the
    A. length of member's service at the time of his death
    B. age of the beneficiary at the time of the member's death
    C. member's age at retirement
    D. member's age at the time of his death

25._____

KEY (CORRECT ANSWERS)

1.	B	11.	A	21.	A
2.	A	12.	A	22.	B
3.	B	13.	A	23.	A
4.	D	14.	D	24.	B
5.	D	15.	A	25.	B
6.	B	16.	A		
7.	A	17.	D		
8.	D	18.	A		
9.	C	19.	D		
10.	D	20.	C		

TEST 2

DIRECTIONS: Each question or incomplete statement is followed by several suggested answers or completions. Select the one that BEST answers the question or completes the statement. *PRINT THE LETTER OF THE CORRECT ANSWER IN THE SPACE AT THE RIGHT.*

Questions 1-4.

DIRECTIONS: Questions 1 through 4 are to be answered SOLELY on the basis of the following passage.

Depreciation -- Any reduction from the upper limit of value. An effect caused by deterioration and/or obsolescence. Deterioration is evidenced by wear and tear, decay, dry rot, cracks, encrustations, or structural defects. Obsolescence is divisible into two parts, functional or economic. Functional obsolescence may be due to poor planning, mechanical inadequacy or overadequacy, functional inadequacy or overadequacy due to size, style, or age. It is evidenced by conditions within the property. Economic obsolescence is caused by changes external to the property, such as neighborhood infiltrations of inharmonious groups or property uses, legislation, etc. It is also the actual decline in market value of the improvement to land from the time of purchase to the time of sale.

1. According to the above passage, a form of physical deterioration can be caused by
    A. termite infestation
    B. zoning regulations
    C. inadequate wiring
    D. extra high ceilings

2. According to the above passage, a form of economic obsolescence may be caused by
    A. structural defects
    B. poor architectural design
    C. changes in zoning regulations
    D. chemical reactions

3. According to the above passage, the statement which BEST explains the meaning of depreciation is that it is a loss in value
    A. caused only by economic obsolescence
    B. resulting from any cause
    C. caused only by wear and tear
    D. resulting from conditions or changes external to the property

4. According to the above passage, the lack of air conditioning in warm climates is
    A. a form of physical deterioration
    B. a form of functional obsolescence
    C. a form of economic obsolescence
    D. not a form of depreciation

Questions 5-8.

DIRECTIONS: Questions 5 through 8 are to be answered SOLELY on the basis of the following passage.

In determining the valuation of income-producing property, the capitalization of income is accepted as a proper approach to value. Income-producing property is bought and sold for the purpose of making money. How much an investor would pay would, of course, depend on how much he could earn on his investment. The amount he would earn on his investment is called a return. The amount of return depends on the degree of risk involved.

If one has $100,000 to invest, it can be put in a bank account at perhaps a 5 percent return. In the bank, the money is relatively safe so the return is lower. If the money were invested by purchasing a block of stores in a depressed area, of course, one would not be satisfied with a 5 percent return. This is what the capitalization of income comes down to - the better the return, the higher the risk. This is the approach an experienced real estate investor uses in determining what he would pay for property.

5. According to the above passage, which one of the following investments would an experienced real estate investor with $100,000 MOST likely choose? A(n)
    A. apartment building in a slum area yielding a 6 percent return
    B. office building rented to professionals yielding a 6 percent return
    C. shopping center in a depressed area yielding a 10 percent return
    D. warehouse rented on a long-term lease to a major corporation yielding a 10 percent return

6. According to the above passage, in the capitalization of income, the relationship between the degree of risk and the rate of return GENERALLY is expected to be
    A. indeterminate   B. variable
    C. inverse   D. direct

7. According to the above passage, in purchasing income-producing property, the one of the following which would NOT be a factor influencing an experienced real estate investor is the
    A. socio-economic characteristics of the area in which the property is located
    B. rate of return on investment
    C. original cost of the property
    D. degree of risk involved

8. According to the above passage, the property listed below which would be LEAST likely to be valued by the capitalization of income is a(n)
    A. apartment house with no vacancies
    B. office building rented to 70 percent of capacity
    C. shopping center with several new tenants
    D. vacant lot located next to a factory

Questions 9-12.

DIRECTIONS: Questions 9 through 12 are to be answered SOLELY on the basis of the following passage.

The cost approach is used by assessors mainly in valuing one-family homes and properties of a special nature which are not commonly bought and sold and do not produce an income.

There are three aspects to the cost approach to valuation. The first is the actual cost of construction. Where the property has recently been built, the cost of constructing the property is relevant. It, however, may not be a true test as to its value. The building may have been constructed so as to serve the special needs of the owner. What it costs to construct may not truly reflect its value; it may be worth more or less. If it is income-producing property, the income may be more or less than expected. It may be sold for more or less than it cost to build.

The second aspect is replacement cost and applies to older structures. It involves the construction of a similar type of building with the same purpose. It does not require the use of the same materials or design.

Reproduction cost is the third aspect, and it also applies to older structures. It involves construction with the exact same materials and design. The cost in the two latter aspects is construction at today's prices with an allowance made for depreciation from the day the original building was constructed.

9. According to the above passage, which one of the following is a CORRECT statement concerning the cost approach to valuation?
   A. In determining value by the replacement and reproduction cost methods, an allowance must be made for depreciation from the day the building was originally constructed.
   B. The cost approach method is the best method to apply in valuing an office building.
   C. When a structure has been recently built, its actual cost is the best method of determining its value.
   D. The fact that a structure has been built to meet the special needs of the occupant is a relevant factor in valuation.

9.____

10. An assessor, in valuing a ten-year-old apartment house, finds that its original construction cost was $1,200,000. In capitalizing its net income, he realizes a valuation of $800,000. In using the replacement cost method and allowing for depreciation, the assessor arrives at a valuation of $900,000.
    According to the above passage, which one of the following valuations is LEAST acceptable for this apartment house?
    A. $1,200,000   B. $800,000
    C. $900,000   D. $850,000

10.____

11. The construction cost of a recently built structure is relevant to value, but may not be a true test of value. According to the above passage, which one of the following statements CORRECTLY explains why this is true?
    A. The builder may not know how to construct economically.
    B. A building can depreciate very quickly.
    C. The building may have been built to satisfy certain unique specifications.
    D. Cost-of-construction is not an accepted method of valuation.

11.____

12. According to the above passage, which one of the following statements CORRECTLY defines the essential difference between the replacement cost and reproduction cost aspects of the cost approach?
    A. Replacement cost is used only in assessing older buildings; reproduction cost is used only when the building has been recently constructed.
    B. Reproduction cost does not include any allowance for depreciation; replacement cost allows for depreciation from the date of construction of the original building.
    C. Replacement cost involves construction with the same exact materials; reproduction cost does not require the use of the same materials.
    D. Reproduction cost involves construction with the exact same materials and design; replacement cost does not require the use of the same materials and design.

Questions 13-18.

DIRECTIONS: Questions 13 through 18 are to be answered SOLELY on the basis of the following passage.

Realty, because of fixity in investment, immobility in location, and necessity for shelter purposes, lends itself readily to economic controls when such are deemed essential to serve social or political ends, or where the interest of health, safety, and morality of community population or the nation at large warrants it. Realty has consistently been recognized as a form of private property which is sufficiently invested with public interest to warrant its control either under the police power of a sovereign state and its branches of government or by direct and statutory legislation enacted within the framework of the governmental constitution.

Whenever war or catastrophe causes a sudden shifting of population or suspension of building operations, or both, an imbalance is brought about in the supply and demand for housing. This imbalance in housing demand and supply creates conditions of insecurity and instability among the tenants who fear indiscriminate eviction or unwarranted upward rental adjustments. It is this background of possible exploitation during times of economic stress and strain that underlies the enactment of emergency rent control legislation.

Although rent control has been in effect in many communities, particularly the larger metropolitan communities, since the end of World War II, the attitude of all levels of government is to view this form of legislation as temporary and to hasten, as far as their power permits, a return to normal relations between landlords and tenants.

13. According to the above passage, the reason that realty can conveniently be subjected to controls is due to
    A. public interest
    B. site immobility
    C. population shifts
    D. moral considerations

14. The above passage includes as a justification for the imposition of economic controls all of the following EXCEPT
    A. threats to physical safety
    B. socio-political considerations
    C. dangers to health in the community
    D. requirements of police powers

15. According to the above passage, a LIKELY cause for a cessation of construction might be a
    A. natural disaster
    B. change in the demand for housing
    C. change in the supply of housing
    D. demographic fluctuations

15._____

16. According to the above passage, of the following, a tenant's insecurity would MOST likely result in his fear of
    A. reduction in necessary services
    B. loss in equity
    C. rent increases
    D. condemnation proceedings

16._____

17. According to the above passage, indiscriminate evictions by landlords during periods of economic difficulties constitute
    A. unlawful acts   B. justifiable measures
    C. desirable actions D. exploitation of tenants

17._____

18. According to the above passage, economic controls of realty have been in effect on a widespread basis since
    A. 1918   B. 1945
    C. 1953   D. 1964

18._____

Questions 19-22.

DIRECTIONS: Questions 19 through 22 are to be answered SOLELY on the basis of the following passage.

In capitalizing the net income of property to produce a value, certain expenses are permitted to be deducted from gross income. Even though the premises may be fully rented, it is proper to deduct from the gross income an allowance for vacancy. All expenses attributable to the maintenance and upkeep of the premises are deductible. These include heat, light and power, water and sewers, wages or employees and expenses attributable to wages, insurance, repairs and maintenance, supplies and materials, legal and accounting fees, telephone, rental commission, advertising, and so forth. If the premises are furnished, a reserve for the depreciation of personal property is deductible. A capital improvement to the building is not a deductible expense. Real estate taxes should not be deducted as an expense. Instead, taxes should be factored as part of the overall capitalization rate.

It is proper to allow an expense for management of the building even in cases where the owner himself is manager. But payments of interest and principal of the mortgage are not a properly deductible expense. Real property is appraised free and clear of all encumbrances. Otherwise, two identical buildings located next to each other might be valued differently because one has a greater mortgage than the other.

19. According to the above passage, the one of the following which is NOT a proper deductible expense during the year in which the expense is incurred is the cost for
    A. advertising to rent the premises
    B. accounting fees
    C. utilities
    D. putting in central air conditioning

20. According to the above passage, the one of the following statements concerning deductible expenses which is CORRECT is that
    A. a vacancy allowance is a proper deductible expense even though the premises may be fully rented
    B. real estate taxes are a proper deductible expense
    C. if the owner manages his own property, he cannot charge a management fee as a deductible expense
    D. payments for interest and principal of the mortgage are proper deductible expenses

21. According to the above passage, two identical adjacent buildings CANNOT receive different valuations because of differences in their
    A. mortgages   B. net income
    C. leases   D. management fees

22. According to the above passage, an owner of furnished premises may set aside a reserve as a deductible expense for all of the following EXCEPT
    A. refrigerators   B. carpeting
    C. bookcases   D. walls

Questions 23-25.

DIRECTIONS: Questions 23 through 25 are to be answered SOLELY on the basis of the following passage.

The standard for assessment in the state is contained in Section 306 of the Real Property Tax Law. It states that all real property in each assessing unit shall be assessed at the full value thereof. However, the courts of the state have not required assessors to assess at 100% of full value. Assessments of property for real estate tax purposes at less than full value are not invalid if they are made at a uniform percentage of full value throughout the assessing district. In assessing real property, full value is equivalent to market value.

In determining market value of real property for tax purposes, every element which can reasonably affect value of property ought to be considered, and the main considerations should be given to actual sales of the subject or similar property, cost to produce or reproduce the property, capitalization of income therefrom, and the combination of these factors.

23. According to the above passage, the one of the following statements which is INCORRECT is that all real property in each assessing unit
    A. must be assessed at full value
    B. shall be assessed at full value or at a uniform percentage of full value
    C. may be assessed at 50% of full value
    D. may be assessed at 100% of full value

24. According to the above passage, the one of the following elements of value which should be given the LEAST consideration in determining market value is
    A. actual or comparable sales
    B. reproduction cost
    C. amount of mortgage
    D. capitalization of income

25. According to the above passage, the basis for the legality of assessing units, making assessments at a uniform percentage of full value rather than at full value is
    A. Section 306 of the Real Property Tax Law
    B. decisions of the state courts
    C. judgments of individual assessors
    D. decisions of municipal executives

KEY (CORRECT ANSWERS)

1.	A	11.	C
2.	C	12.	D
3.	B	13.	B
4.	B	14.	D
5.	D	15.	A
6.	D	16.	C
7.	C	17.	D
8.	D	18.	B
9.	A	19.	D
10.	A	20.	A

21.	A
22.	D
23.	A
24.	C
25.	B

TEST 3

DIRECTIONS: Each question or incomplete statement is followed by several suggested answers or completions. Select the one that BEST answers the question or completes the statement. *PRINT THE LETTER OF THE CORRECT ANSWER IN THE SPACE AT THE RIGHT.*

Questions 1-4.

DIRECTIONS: Questions 1 through 4 are to be answered SOLELY on the basis of the following passage.

Although zoning is a phase of city planning and is concerned with land use control of private property, zoning powers are better known and more generally applied than most city planning powers. Zoning powers predict the formulation of a master plan and even the formation of the planning commission itself. The widespread application of zoning powers is evident from a survey conducted by the International City Managers' Association. As reported in the 2015 MUNICIPAL YEARBOOK, 98 percent of all cities in excess of ten thousand population had enacted comprehensive zoning ordinances governing the utilization of privately owned land. Since 60 percent of all urban land is generally held under private ownership, the impact of zoning laws upon income and value of real property is most significant.

1. According to the above passage, in relation to the powers of city planning, zoning powers are
    - A. not as familiar to the general public
    - B. formulated subsequent to the establishment of the powers of the planning commission
    - C. more general in their application
    - D. likely to develop as a result of the community's master plan

1._____

2. According to the above passage, if there are 200 cities in the United States with a population exceeding 10,000 persons, the number of such cities LIKELY to have enacted comprehensive zoning laws is
    - A. 190
    - B. 192
    - C. 194
    - D. 196

2._____

3. According to the above passage, for each 400 acres of urban land, it is LIKELY that the amount of land which would be privately owned would be _____ acres.
    - A. 220
    - B. 240
    - C. 260
    - D. 280

3._____

4. Of the following, the one whose land use is MOST likely to be affected by zoning controls, according to the above passage, is
    - A. Sears Department Store
    - B. the Port Authority terminal
    - C. the New York Public Library at 42nd Street
    - D. the Federal Building

4._____

Questions 5-7.

DIRECTIONS: Questions 5 through 7 are to be answered SOLELY on the basis of the following passage.

Apartments located in rehabilitated old law tenement houses are designated as *off-site apartments*. The purpose of such apartments is to provide temporary housing accommodations for the relocation of persons and families living on sites which are to be used for future housing projects who can not otherwise be relocated. A family shall be permitted to continue to occupy an off-site apartment for a period of two years from the date of its admission and shall be required to move out at the termination of such two-year period. However, no proceedings shall be undertaken to remove any tenant now in occupancy of an off-site apartment until after May 9, 2015.

A family shall, however, be required to remove from an off-site apartment prior to the expiration of the periods and date enumerated above if it refuses to accept an available apartment in a public housing project for which it is eligible; or, as a tenant in occupancy, it fails to execute any lease required by management or it fails to comply with other requirements, standard procedures, or rules promulgated by management.

5. A tenant occupying an off-site apartment refuses to renew his lease for one year because he expects to move into a new apartment house within six months. This tenant may
   A. be required to move before his new apartment is ready
   B. be required to move before his new apartment is ready only if his occupancy in the off-site apartment exceeds two years
   C. not be required to move before his new apartment is ready
   D. not be required to move prior to May 9, 2015

6. According to the above passage, if a family living on a site can be relocated to an apartment in a public housing project, it is
   A. eligible for an off-site apartment near its present dwelling
   B. not eligible for any off-site apartment
   C. eligible for an off-site apartment if it has been living in its present home for at least two years
   D. permitted to continue in occupancy for at least two more years

7. According to the above passage, a tenant admitted to an off-site apartment on October 1, 2013 is FIRST subject to removal after
   A. October 1, 2015
   B. May 9, 2015
   C. he has been investigated and found to be ineligible for an apartment in the public housing project
   D. he refuses to sign a lease on the apartment or after September 30, 2015, whichever comes first

Questions 8-14.

DIRECTIONS: Questions 8 through 14 are to be answered SOLELY on the basis of the following passage.

From a nationwide point of view, the need for new housing units during the years immediately ahead will be determined by four major factors. The most important factor is the net change in household formations -- that is, the difference between the number of new households that are formed and the number of existing households that are dissolved, whether by death or other circumstances. During the 2010's, as the children born during the '80's and 90's come of age and marry, the total number of households is expected to increase at a rate of more than 1,000,000 annually. The second factor affecting the need for new housing units is *removals* -- that is, existing units that are demolished, damaged beyond repair, or otherwise removed from the housing supply. A third factor is the number of existing vacancies. To some extent, vacancies can satisfy the housing demand caused by increases in total number of households or by removals, although population shifts that are already underway mean that some areas will have a surfeit of vacancies and other areas will be faced with serious shortages of housing. A final factor, and one that has only recently assumed major importance, is the increasing demand for second homes. These may take any form from a shack in the woods for a city dweller to a pied-a-terre in the city for a suburbanite. Whatever the form, however, it is certain that increasing leisure time, rising amounts of discretionary income, and improvements in transportation are leading more and more Americans to look on a second home not as a rich man's luxury but as the common man's right.

8. The above passage uses the term *housing units* to refer to
   A. residences of all kinds
   B. apartment buildings only
   C. one-family houses only
   D. the total number of families in the United States

9. The above passage uses the word *removals* to mean
   A. the shift of population from one area to another
   B. vacancies that occur when families move
   C. financial losses suffered when a building is damaged or destroyed
   D. former dwellings that are demolished or can no longer be used for housing

10. The expression *pied-a-terre* appears in the next-to-last sentence in the above passage.
    A person who is not familiar with the expression should be able to tell from the way it is used here that it PROBABLY means
    A. a suburban home owned by a commuter
    B. a shack in the woods
    C. a second home that is used from time to time
    D. overnight lodging for a traveler in a strange city

11. Of the factors described in the above passage as having an important influence on the demand for housing, which factor, taken alone, is LEAST likely to encourage the construction of new housing?
    The
    A. net change in household formations
    B. destruction of existing housing
    C. existence of vacancies
    D. use of second homes

12. Based on the above passage, the TOTAL increase in the number of households during the 2010's is expected to be MOST NEARLY
    A. 1,000,000   B. 10,000,000
    C. 100,000,000   D. 1,000,000,000

13. Which one of the following conclusions could MOST logically be drawn from the information given in the above passage?
    A. The population of the United States is increasing at the rate of about 1,000,000 people annually.
    B. There is already a severe housing shortage in all parts of the country.
    C. The need for additional housing units is greater in some parts of the country than in others.
    D. It is still true that only wealthy people can afford to keep up more than one home.

14. Which one of the following conclusions could NOT logically be drawn from the information given in the above passage?
    A. The need for new housing will be even greater in the 2020's than in the 2010's.
    B. Demolition of existing housing must be taken into account in calculating the need for new housing construction.
    C. Having a second home is more common today than it was in the 1970's.
    D. Part of the housing needs of the 2010's can be met by vacancies.

Questions 15-18.

DIRECTIONS: Questions 15 through 18 are to be answered SOLELY on the basis of the following passage.

A city may expand by growing vertically through the replacement of lower buildings with higher ones; or by filling in open spaces between settled areas; or by extending the existing settled area. When the settled area is expanded, growth may take several forms, the most important forms being concentric circle or ring growth around the central nucleus; axial growth, with prongs or fingerlike extensions moving out along main transportation routes; and suburban growth, with the establishment of islands of settlements before the expansion of the main city area. These types of expansion are characteristic of most large cities. Baltimore was for a long time a good example of ring growth, whereas New York, Chicago, and Detroit illustrate axial and suburban growth.

15. The title that BEST expresses the theme of the above passage is
    A. FORMS OF CITY EXPANSION
    B. MAJOR METROPOLITAN PROBLEMS
    C. METHODS OF URBAN PLANNING
    D. SUBURBAN GROWTH IN AMERICA

16. The one of the following which is an example of vertical growth is the
    A. settlement of year-round residents along the upper Hudson River
    B. restoration of former rooming houses to their original brownstone condition
    C. subdivision of large estates into small lot semidetached houses
    D. erection of the Empire State Building in New York City

17. A city that grew as a concentric circle is
    A. Baltimore   B. New York
    C. Chicago   D. Detroit

18. When the author speaks of axial growth, he refers to a situation where 18._____
    A. expansion is primarily into rural areas until suburbs are thereby created
    B. small towns and villages are consolidated by gradually growing until one large city is created
    C. the direction in which a city expands is determined by the location of major highways
    D. the number of new buildings is greater than the number of old buildings demolished

Questions 19-21.

DIRECTIONS: Questions 19 through 21 are to be answered SOLELY on the basis of the following passage.

Incentive zoning is an affirmative tool that has widespread applications. The Zoning Resolution which became effective in 1998 substantially reduced the amount of floor space that a developer could put up on a given size lot and increased the light and air. In the Trump Building, which was built under the old legislation, the floor space is 27 times the size of the lot. The maximum ratio allowed for buildings now without a special permit is 18.

The 1998 zoning ordinance provided incentives to developers to devote part of the plot to public plazas or arcades. This space is needed to supplement the sidewalks, which in many cases are as narrow as they were when the midtown area was lined with brownstone or brickfront houses.

While the newer zoning has produced plazas, it has not of itself proved to be a sufficient development control. Stretches of Third Avenue and the Avenue of the Americas, for example, have been almost completely redeveloped in the last few years. This massive private investment has produced several fine individual buildings. The total environment produced, however, has been disappointing in a number of respects, and there is nowhere near the amenity that there could have been.

19. According to the above passage, the use of incentive zoning has NOT been entirely successful because it 19._____
    A. has discouraged redevelopment
    B. has encouraged massive private development along Third Avenue
    C. has been ineffective in controlling overall redevelopment
    D. has not significantly increased the number of parks and plazas being built

20. According to the above passage, one might conclude that before the 1998 Zoning Resolution was passed, 20._____
    A. buildings on a given site were required to have greater setbacks
    B. the amount of private investment in development was significantly smaller than it is today
    C. no controls on development existed
    D. the provision of parks and plazas was less frequent

21. In the context of the above passage, the word *amenity* means 21.____
    A. compliance with regulations
    B. correction of undesirable environmental aspects
    C. responsiveness to guidelines and incentives
    D. pleasant or desirable features

Questions 22-24.

DIRECTIONS: Questions 22 through 24 are to be answered SOLELY on the basis of the following passage.

Physical design plays a very significant role in crime rate. Crime rate has been found to increase almost proportionately with building height. The average number of crimes is much greater in higher buildings than in lower ones (equal to or less than six stories). What is most interesting is that in buildings of six stories or less, the project size or total number of units does not make a difference. It seems that although larger projects encourage crime by fostering feelings of anonymity, isolation, irresponsibility, and lack of identity with surroundings, evidence indicates that larger projects encompassed in low buildings seem to offset what we may assume to be factors conducive to high crime rates. High-rise projects not only experience a higher rate of crime within the buildings, but a greater proportion of the crime occurs in the interior public spaces of these buildings as compared with those of the lower buildings. Lower buildings have more limited public space than higher ones. A criminal probably perceives that the interior public areas of buildings are where his victims are most vulnerable and where the possibility of his being seen or apprehended is minimal. Placement of elevators, entrance lobbies, fire stairs, and secondary exits all are factors related to the likelihood of crimes taking place in buildings. The study of all of these elements should bear some weight in the planning of new projects.

22. According to the above passage, which of the following BEST describes the relationship between building size and crime? 22.____
    A. Larger projects lead to a greater crime rate.
    B. Higher buildings tend to increase the crime rate.
    C. The smaller the number of project apartments in low buildings, the higher the crime rate.
    D. Anonymity and isolation serve to lower the crime rate in small buildings.

23. According to the above passage, the likelihood of a criminal attempting a mugging in the interior public portions of a high-rise building is GOOD because 23.____
    A. tenants will be constantly flowing in and out of the area
    B. there is easy access to fire stairs and secondary exits
    C. there is a good chance that no one will see him
    D. tenants may not recognize the victims of crime as their neighbors

24. Which of the following is IMPLIED by the above passage as an explanation for the fact that the crime rate is lower in large low-rise housing projects than in large high-rise projects?
    A. Tenants know each other better and take a greater interest in what happens in the project.
    B. There is more public space where tenants are likely to gather together.
    C. The total number of units in a low-rise project is fewer than the total number of units in a high-rise project.
    D. Elevators in low-rise buildings travel quickly, thus limiting the amount of time in which a criminal can act.

24._____

25. The financing of housing represents two distinct forms of costs. One is the actual capital invested, and the other is the interest rate which is charged for the use of capital. In fixing rents, the interest rate which capital is expected to yield plays a very important part. On the basis of this statement, it would be MOST correct to state that
    A. the financing of housing represents two distinct forms of capital investment
    B. reducing the interest rate charged for the use of capital is not as important as economies in construction in achieving lower rentals
    C. in fixing rents, the interest rate is expected to yield capital gains, justifying the investment
    D. the actual capital invested and the interest rate charged for use of this capital are factors in determining housing costs

25._____

KEY (CORRECT ANSWERS)

1.	C	11.	C
2.	D	12.	B
3.	B	13.	C
4.	A	14.	A
5.	A	15.	A
6.	B	16.	D
7.	D	17.	A
8.	A	18.	C
9.	D	19.	C
10.	C	20.	D

21.	D
22.	B
23.	C
24.	A
25.	D

LAND DEVELOPMENT

CONTENTS

	Page
I. COMMUNITY CENTERS	1
Size	1
Location	1
Access	2
Number of access points	3
Access-point design	4
Site design	7
Parking	10
II. WORK SITES	12
Parking demand	13
Peak-hour demand	13
Site selection	13
Parking design	14

LAND DEVELOPMENT

COMMUNITY CENTERS WORK SITES

LAND DEVELOPMENT DETERMINES ROAD NEEDS

Land use, to a large extent, **determines road needs.** Therefore, any change in land use should be evaluated to determine its probable effect on the road system. The evaluation should answer two basic questions: "*Will the new development create congestion or unsafe conditions on adjacent streets?*" and "*Will the new development have adequate off-street parking?*"

Most small developments will not generate enough traffic to create capacity-related congestion. However, this may not be true for community centers, large office buildings, commissaries, exchanges, and hospitals. This chapter provides guidance for evaluating access and parking design for these facilities.

I. COMMUNITY CENTER

A community center is a group of commercial establishments planned and developed to maximize the sale of goods and provision of services. This grouping of related activities on one site, with common access and off-street parking facilities, benefits both tenants and patrons and has proved to be a successful marketing concept. However, these centers generate heavy traffic volumes, which require a sophisticated design for site access and external roadways to accommodate the traffic demand.

SIZE

On military installations, there are two basic types of centers: **neighborhood and community. Neighborhood centers** sell daily living needs (food, drugs, sundries, and personal services). They include from 5 to 15 stores, require at least 1,000 families for support, and need from 5 to 10 acres of land.

Community centers generally contain a major exchange, commissary, bank, credit union, theater, snack bar, cafeteria, post office, bowling alley, service station, package store, barber and beauty shops, and laundry. They usually require at least 5,000 families and a site area of 15 to 30 acres.

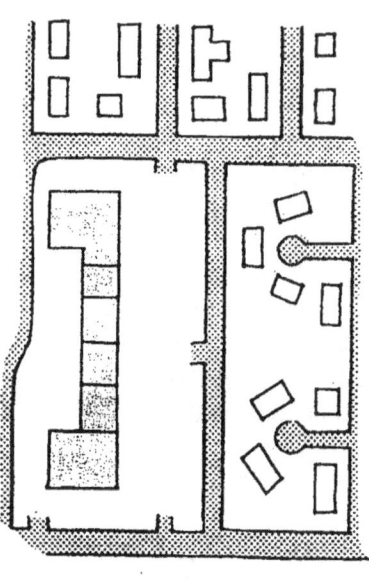

NEIGHBORHOOD

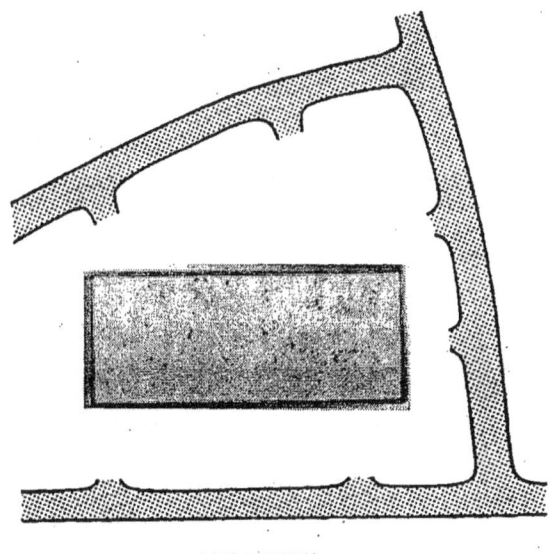

COMMUNITY

LOCATION

The **community center** should be **conveniently located with respect to a majority of its potential customers**. It should be accessible to both vehicular and pedestrian traffic; it must not be bisected by through roads.

In site selection, the land area should be large enough for proposed buildings, adequate parking facilities, and buffer zones. The site should be a single parcel, regular in shape, with generally level or gently sloping topography, safe from flooding, and without excessive drainage problems. Odd-shaped sites and rough terrain should be avoided, because they not only require contrived layouts and additional construction cost for multilevel parking areas, but they also decrease the ease of traffic circulation. Also, the land area should not require excessive fill, particularly in the area to be occupied by buildings. In every case, the bearing quality of the subsoil should be determined prior to site selection.

ACCESS

The **greatest impact of community center traffic** is generally at the site itself and on the roadways that provide direct access to the site. Therefore, analysis of traffic impact usually can be limited to the number, location, and type of access points required. A major factor in determining this requirement is the expected daily traffic pattern to and from the center. This pattern is related to the center's size, operating hours, trade area, and to patron habits.

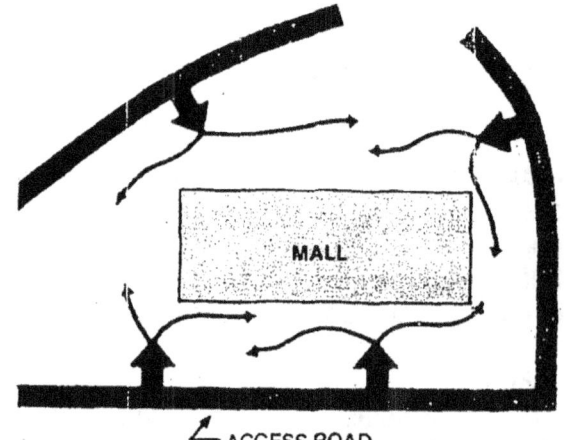

FACTORS INFLUENCING ACCESS-POINT

Amount of site frontage available for access facilities. Access to more than one major street from large centers should be provided to ensure a balanced distribution of center-generated traffic volumes.

Traffic volumes generated by the center, as well as through volumes on adjacent streets. Analysis of abutting streets for access should determine not only their ability to handle center traffic, but also the desirability of using these streets for access.

Directional distribution of center traffic approaching and departing. Unbalanced patterns are usual and should be considered when designing for turning movements.

Location and geometrics of existing cross streets and relationships to existing and future intersection spacing. If possible, existing signalized intersections should be used for access to the center. Use of these intersections can prevent possible undesirable spacing of intersections, particularly if the new access would require signalization. On the other hand, these advantages must be weighed against possible delays caused by overloading of the intersection.

Access needs of land uses adjacent to the center. When developing land around community centers, driveways for separate mall facilities (bank, service station, and so forth) should not be connected individually and directly to the major access road. If these facilities are located on the main site, the access drives should be connected to the community center internal circulation system. If they are opposite the major road providing access to the site, the drives should be aligned opposite the major community center entrances. Excessive driveways, connected individually to the access road, create traffic congestion, increase accidents, and reduce capacity. Planners should be careful not to concentrate too much activity and overload the road system.

NUMBER OF ACCESS POINTS

$$ACCESS\ DRIVES = \frac{PROJECTED\ TRIPS}{CAPACITY\ OF\ SINGLE\ ACCESS}$$

Site frontage determines the number of access points that can be provided; however, the number of access points actually provided should be based on the volume of traffic generated and the capability of each access point to serve traffic. When traffic pattern distribution is doubtful, more access points than appear to be necessary for capacity purposes should be provided.

A major factor in determining the number of access points required is the volume of traffic generated. Because of the many variables affecting traffic generation, standard rates have not been developed. However, for preliminary planning, one-way trip-generation factors of between 5 and 15 vehicle trips per hour per 1,000 square feet of gross floor area are applicable. The higher rate should be used for the smaller center and also where there is a high turnover; the lower rate is more appropriate for the larger centers. An average of 10 one-way trips per hour per 1,000 square feet of gross floor area is suggested for the average community center.

After the volume of traffic that will be generated by the center has been determined and before the number of required access points can be determined, **the capacity of a single access point must be known.** This capacity can vary widely, depending on access design, vehicle loadings, adjacent roadways, and traffic control and distribution. Criteria for determining intersection capacity, as explained in the 1965 Highway Capacity Manual, should be used for this evaluation. In this analysis, peak-hour volumes are the most critical. Peak-travel periods for most installation roadways are between 0700 and 0900 and 1600 and 1800 hours and are primarily work-related trips. Therefore, for centers that open between 0900 and 1800 hours, the peak-hour traffic may coincide with the work-related peak flows. This period would then represent the critical time frame for which street requirements should be examined and designed.

ACCESS-POINT DESIGN

The type of traffic movements to be made determines ACCESS-POINT DESIGN. In this section, typical designs for resolving access problems are shown, and design principles are given.

DESIGN GUIDES

- Access points should be designed to serve pedestrians and bicycles as well as automobiles. Many community centers are built near residential areas where non driver segments are not uncommon. Marked walkways, precautionary signing, grade-separated structures, and special crosswalk lighting are applicable protection measures for these segments.

- Driveways to handle a moderate number of left turns without signal control should have two outbound lanes; one for right turns and one for left turns. Dual turning lanes should be used only with signal control.

- Driveway cross sections may vary from a minimum one-way-in or one-way-out drive, 14 to 16 feet wide, to a maximum of four inbound and four outbound lanes. Where more than one inbound and one outbound lane is provided, a median divider at least 4 feet wide is desirable. Median widths in excess of 16 feet are generally undesirable; they create turning problems and give the access drive a larger opening on the street.

- A minimum 15-foot turning radius is essential at access points, with 25- to 50-foot radii desirable.

- Caution should be used in developing barrier channelization; too much can be a hazard.

- Basic vehicular storage requirements should be determined for each access point. On the street serving inbound traffic, left- and right-turn storage is generally critical. Inadequate storage for inbound movements will result in traffic backups onto the through lanes, reducing through-traffic capacity. For traffic exiting the center, left turns are usually the critical movement. An inadequate outbound storage lane can result in backups onto the center's internal circulation road.

TYPICAL ACCESS DESIGNS

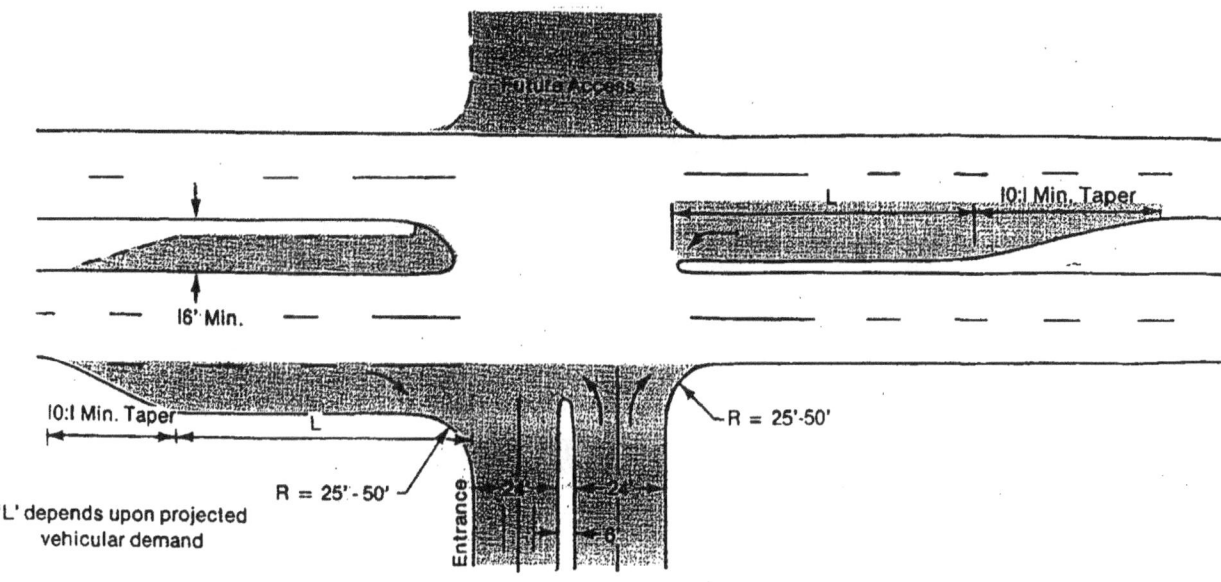

This design is the most commonly used treatment for a major entrance/exit drive. As noted in the figure, it is desirable to locate access facilities for undeveloped properties opposite the existing center's access. This allows for efficient signalization and overall safe traffic operation.

The divided cross section of the entrance provides the desired separation. As shown, the turning radii of 25 to 50 feet will permit higher turning speeds; however, if pedestrian movements are a consideration, smaller radii may be desirable. Protected left turn storage lanes are provided to separate left turning traffic from through traffic. The length of the storage lane is based on a capacity analysis. The transition taper should not be less than 10:1, and the storage lanes should be at least 12 feet wide.

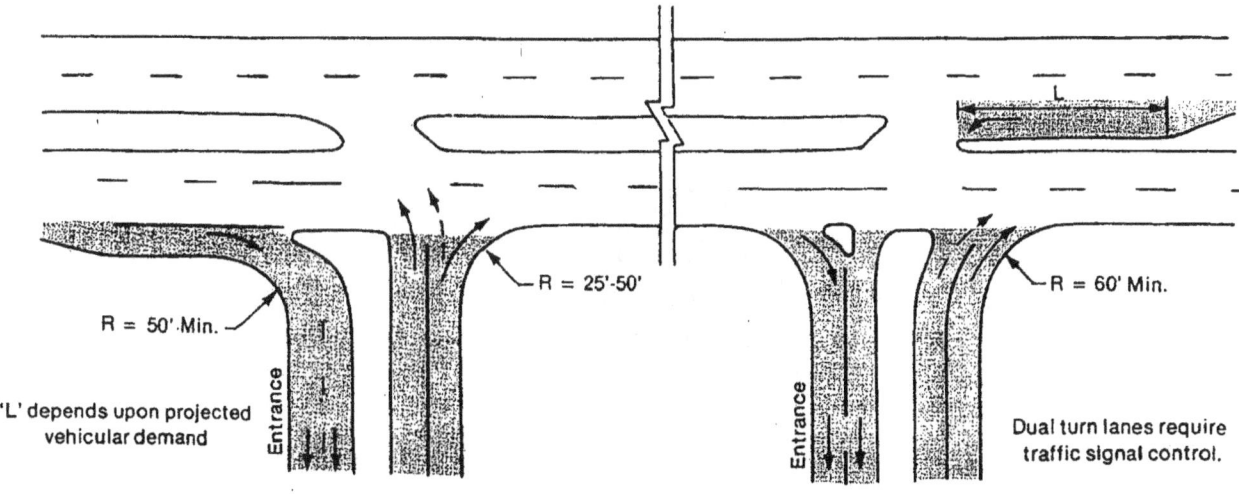

Shown in this design are directional entrance/exits that can be used for major inbound/outbound movements. The design would best serve where drivers have limited access to other entrances and thus, the use of the entrance serving each direction is maximized. Skewing of entrances can enhance operation and increase capacity.

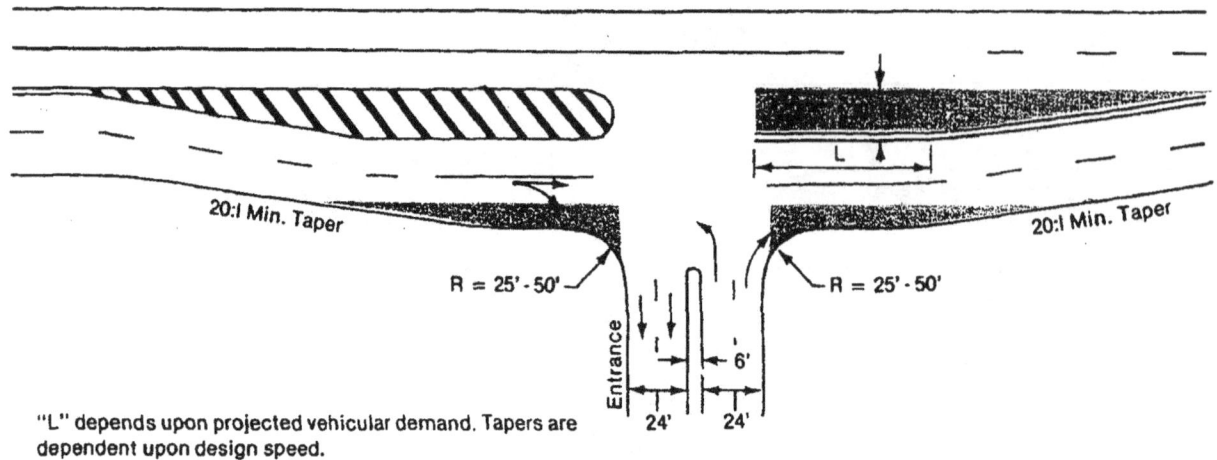

"L" depends upon projected vehicular demand. Tapers are dependent upon design speed.

Left-turn storage on an undivided route created by road widening is shown in this design. Although the roadway is shown widened on the entrance drive side, the widening may be on the opposite side or equal on both sides.

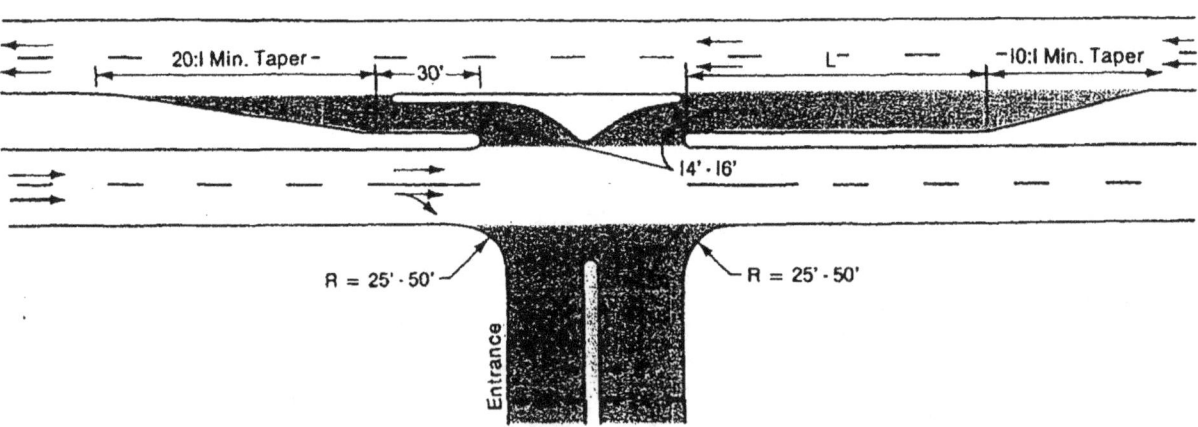

"L" depends upon projected vehicular demand. Tapers are dependent upon design speed.

This design illustrates a left-turn treatment for use on a major road with a median wider than 20 feet. It may also be used successfully on two-lane roadways where adequate width is available to flare the intersection.

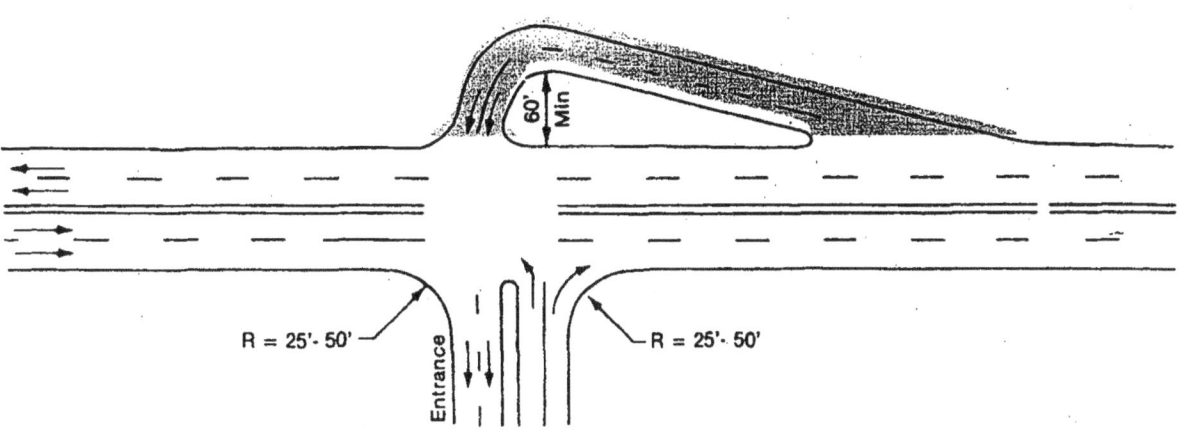

This jug handle design provides high left turn capacity and usually requires less right of way than a dual left turn

SITE DESIGN

A PRINCIPAL OBJECTIVE OF SITE DESIGN should be to bring the patron close to as many facilities as possible once the person emerges from the automobile and becomes a pedestrian.

The capability of a new development to meet this objective depends, to a large degree, on the building arrangement.

Location of buildings generally is determined by site shape, topography, access to abutting streets, use of existing structures, number and size of buildings, construction costs, and personal preference. However, **the center** generally takes one of the following forms: **strip, court, mall, or cluster**. Variations of these basic layouts can be adapted for any type of center. Usually, the strip and court layouts are most suitable for the smaller shopping centers.

BASIC SITE DESIGNS

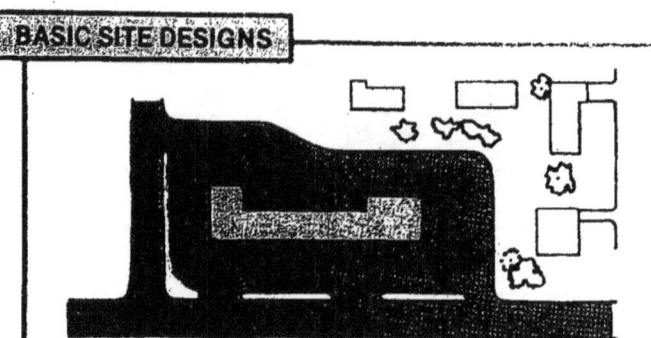

STRIP — simple lines of stores most economical for small centers.

COURT OR U — layout creates natural key store locations at ends and center, adapting to rectangular, square, or corner plots.

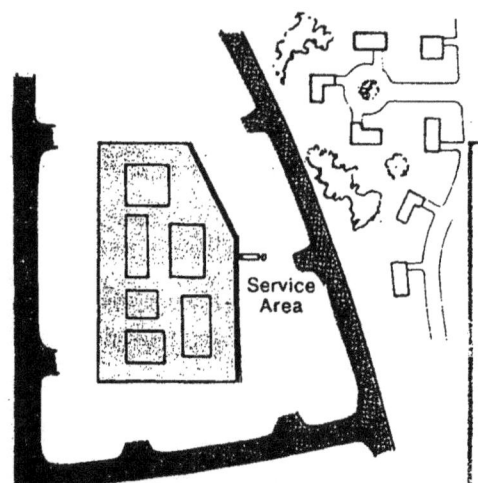

GROUP OR CLUSTER — used essentially for large centers and, with careful planning, can produce an integrated center on nearly any property.

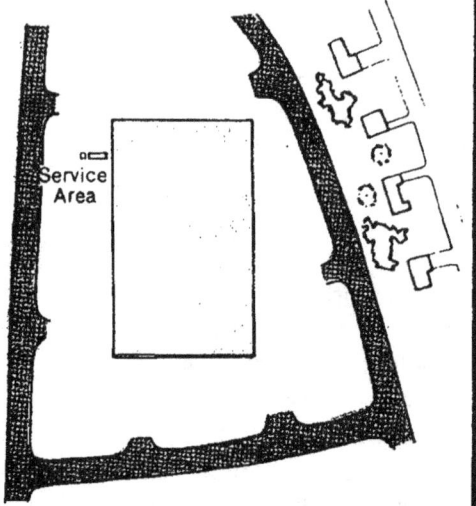

MALL — results in better equalization in store locations, and is good for centralized utility service with service access to stores provided by a truck tunnel under the mall (or service courts).

ARRANGEMENT OF BUILDINGS

- Stores requiring a large number of parking spaces should be placed far apart when possible.

- Shops complementing each other, such as retail stores offering shopping goods, should be located close together for convenience and comparison. Other separate groupings should include convenience outlets and service facilities. Food stores, especially commissaries, should be well separated from comparison shopping outlets.

- Service offices should be located to one side or apart from the main body of the shopping center so that shoppers and persons seeking services mix as little as possible.

- Service stations in community centers are fitting and proper if their locations do not interfere with circulation in the parking lot. Stations should usually be located in a prominent place.

- All community centers should be readily accessible to potential customers. If a large number of customers are contemplated, the center should be located near more than one important roadway.

- Often it is desirable or necessary to build a community center by stages. In this case, the best design for a particular location and size often must be modified to allow stage construction. Increased building area must be served by adequate parking facilities.

PARKING

OFF-STREET PARKING AREAS are essential to all community centers. Parking facilities may be located entirely in front of or entirely at the rear of the buildings, or they may be • both in front of and at the rear of the buildings. In some cases, they are on all sides. The decision as to where to locate parking depends on the relative importance of planned shopping and impulse shopping. It has been estimated that peak-load parking conditions occur only 15 to 20 percent of the open-store time. Thus, a relatively small proportion of parking facilities in front of the stores will accommodate all customers most of the time.

PARKING LAYOUT

- For shopper convenience, parking should be no more than 300 to 350 feet from a building.
- Parking rows should be perpendicular to buildings for the safety and convenience of pedestrians; however, perpendicular rows less than 130 feet long are not practical. In this case, use rows parallel to the front of the store.
- Employee and customer parking should not mix; therefore, separate parking facilities should be provided for employees.
- Pedestrian crossing points should be kept to a minimum, should be well marked and lighted, and should lead directly to the store groups.
- Occasionally, covered walkways extending into major parking areas are desirable; such walkways should be lighted for nighttime use and may be landscaped.

PARKING ⟹
1. NUMBER OF STALLS
2. SIZE OF STALLS
3. OTHER PARKING NEEDS

1. NUMBER OF STALLS

Generally accepted practice has shown that parking facilities should be designed to accommodate all but the 10 highest shopping hours (usually in the pre-Christmas or pre-Easter seasons). The design to accommodate this period would represent a functionally and economically sound level of parking service.

General guidelines for determining the number of required parking spaces are 5 to 10 car spaces per 1,000 feet of gross building space or 2 to 4 square feet of parking space per square foot of gross building space.

In the first method, the required area does not include driveways. The second method provides 400 square feet per car, allocating between 180 and 200 square feet to the parking space; the remaining area is allocated to access and interior drives, and to landscaped and unusable areas. The selection of either method depends on the proportion of auto to walk-in shoppers and on the ratio of gross building space to retail sales area.

2. SIZE OF STALLS

Dimensions or the various parking and aisle arrangements depend on the parking angle and traffic circulation. However, where room is available, stalls should be 10 feet wide, but never less than 9 feet wide. Double-line stall separators, 1-foot apart, are preferable to single-line stall separators for high-turnover parking as they insure better vehicle positioning in the stall. Aisles that accommodate heavy circulation movements should be 10 feet wider than those normally required.

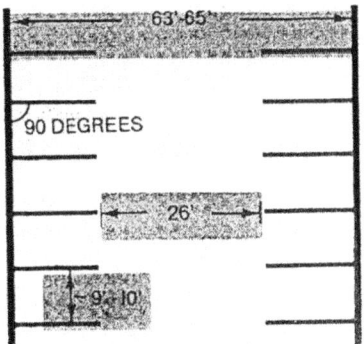

3. OTHER PARKING NEEDS

LOT CIRCULATION

Direction or traffic flow through a community center is a matter of preference and is influenced by the layout of the buildings. Although two-way movement is preferred by the patron, one-way movement is more efficient; however, neither movement appears to be safer than the other. Also, parking directly in front of stores, which is convenient for patrons, influences lot circulation by creating congestion.

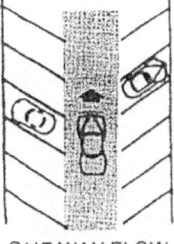 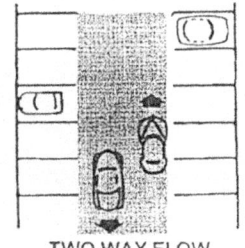

ONE-WAY FLOW   TWO-WAY FLOW

TRUCK SERVICE AREAS

In the layout of truck service areas and truck access roads, every effort should be made to keep them separate from pedestrian areas and customer parking. However, truck service areas, such as in the strip layout, can be made to the rear of the buildings. Service courts can be used efficiently for service with all layouts. In a cluster-type center, truck service easily can be provided in the center of the cluster. However, truck service to a mall design cannot be to the center or to the outside without customer-service conflict and unsightliness. The best, but most costly, truck service for a mall is by tunnel to the building basements. In layouts where truck and patron mixing cannot be avoided, the problem can be minimized by rigid control of time allocation for in and out truck delivery. However, this method is likely to prove inadequate.

LANDSCAPING

Although the essential purpose of the center is to provide shops and services for the patron, landscaping makes a valuable contribution. The objective of landscaping should be to create focal points of beauty, to provide a buffer zone between adjacent land uses, and to subdivide large parking areas.

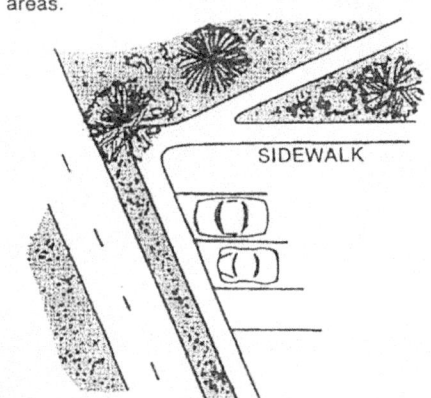

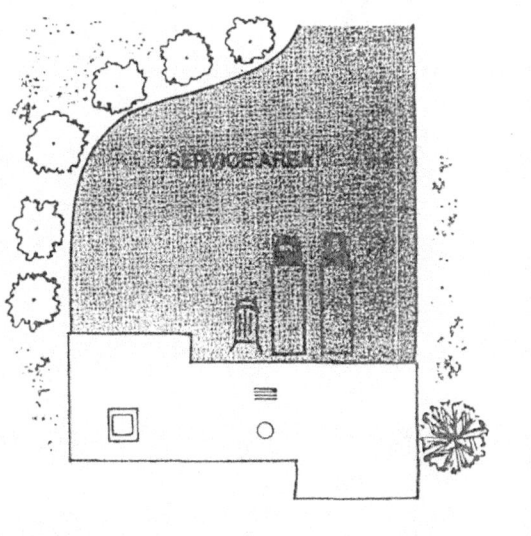

II. *WORK SITES*

The problem of providing adequate parking facilities for employees is one that should concern both the installation planner and the individual worker. At existing facilities, many signs point to inadequate employee parking. Most give clear evidence of unsafe and inefficient conditions that can be corrected.

Overflow parking occurs in driveways, on-streets, and in other available but unauthorized places. With this unregulated parking, pick-up areas for carpool members or for cars driven by employee family members often are inadequate. Illegal parking in aisles, disregard of directional signs and markings, and vacant parking stalls, indicate inefficient design. Improperly designed sidewalks, crosswalks, loading zones, and parking locations encourage conflicts between pedestrians and vehicles. Long delays at entrances and exits, and long walking distances encourage unsafe driver and pedestrian practices.

PARKING DEMAND
DESIGN PARKING DEMAND TO ACCOMMODATE 70% OF THE EMPLOYMENT

Traffic generation, as discussed in chapter 3, can be used to determine the peak volume of cars to be parked and the peak volume of traffic to be moved onto the installation road network. PARKING DEMAND AT A WORK LOCATION is defined as **the maximum accumulation of vehicles parked** at one time. Because parking demand correlates well with employment, the number of employees may be used to predict demand. The relationship of parking demand to employment is generally around 0.6 spaces per employee. However, for design, a yardstick value of 0.7 spaces per employee is desirable. This higher ratio allows supply to exceed demand, thus reducing the search for the last available space. If it takes too long to find a space, the employee will park illegally.

PARKING ESTIMATES

- Obtain employment by category: executive, Office, operational.
- Estimate parking requirements of each employment category, considering transit usage and car occupancy.
- Analyze shift start and end times to determine maximum parking demand.
- Allow a contingency of 5 to 10 percent for seasonal fluctuation, inefficient space usage, overtime schedules, and visitor parking.

THE PEAK-HOUR DEMAND

DESIGN PARKING DEMA ND TO ACCOMMODATE 70% OF THE EMPLOYMENT

THE PEAK-HOUR DEMAND at a work location is essential in estimating the traffic impact on the adjacent street system and in providing efficient ingress and egress. **The peak-hour demand** can be expressed as a proportion of vehicles per maximum shift employee. For design purposes, an estimate of 0.4 to 0.6 vehicles per maximum shift employee arriving in the peak hour can be used to estimate traffic demand. If shifts are not staggered, the higher figure is generally appropriate. On the other hand, the lower hourly rate is more suitable where shifts are staggered.

SITE SELECTION

Among the many factors influencing the choice of a work site that of employee parking and access should not be overlooked. Employee on-street parking reduces street capacity and is a hindrance to traffic flow; therefore, sufficient space should be available to provide off-street parking. When assessing work locations, it should be remembered that employee travel has an important influence on the street system.

Where possible, major facilities should be located on collector streets, and employee traffic should not use local residential streets. Also, the number and location of entrance/exit drives depend on the external roadway system as well as on the internal lot circulation. It may be desirable or even necessary, to distribute peak-hour volumes among several streets to avoid overtaxing the capacity of nearby intersections.

14

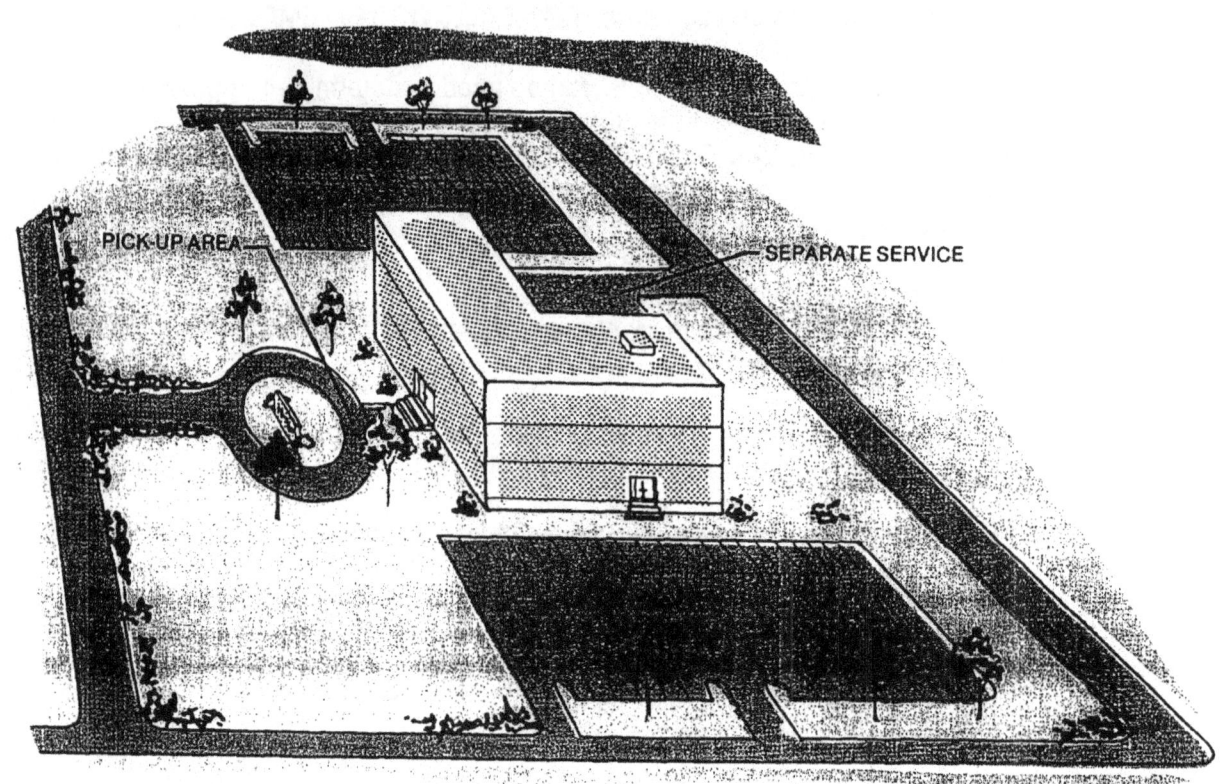

PARKING DESIGN

Unlike parking at community centers, **employee parking is long-term** and is characterized by the nearly simultaneous arrival and departure of many vehicles and by brief periods of vehicle-pedestrian conflict.

Vehicle dimensions are the principal determinant of stall size. Current practice is to employ 9-foot-wide stalls, with 10 foot-wide stalls in some 90-degree visitor parking layouts. If stall widths are less than 9 feet, double lines between stalls should be used to assure better positioning of vehicles.

Stall lengths must be at least 18 feet; however, if drive-through parking is used, stall lengths may be increased to 19 feet to allow for clearance between vehicles. Clearance from walls, fences, roadways, or walkways can be maintained by using curbs or wheel-stops properly positioned within the stall area. A front overhang of 3 feet and a rear overhang of 5 feet are typical.

Decisions on the angle of stall and the layout of aisles must be based on individual site conditions, such as placement and number of entrances and exits, and on site shape and contour. For large parking areas, blocks limiting parking to between 300 and 500 cars are preferable to larger blocks. Pedestrian-vehicle conflicts can be reduced, and assigned parking can be better controlled through use of relatively small blocks.

15
PEDESTRIAN NEEDS

- Allocate parking space to specific buildings.
- Design parking areas to avoid crossing major roads and to include major walkways.
- Designate major crosswalks by pavement markings, signs, flashing lights, or traffic signals, depending on pedestrian and vehicular volumes. To make them visible to drivers, crosswalk surfaces may be raised slightly unless drainage problems would result.
- Arrange parking aisles to lead directly to buildings. This layout will minimize inbound problems since proximate spaces will be taken first and late arrivals will park farther away. Pedestrians can then walk past parked cars rather than cross aisles when arriving motorists are parking.
- Construct overpasses or underpasses at key crossing points. Grade separation may be essential to prevent long delays and time losses. For example, they may be necessary where parking facilities and office buildings are on opposite sides of a major roadway and also where intersection capacity problems preclude pedestrian phases in traffic signals. However, before such facilities are constructed, careful analysis should be made to determine if they are warranted and if, when constructed, they would be used.

GLOSSARY OF CAD/DRAFTING TERMS

2D plane: A flat, infinite 2D surface.

A

active standard: The standard that is currently in use in a model or drawing file.

aligned dimension: A dimension used to define an object or feature that is not vertical or horizontal.

alt-drag: Establishing assembly constraints, including mate, flush, tangent, and insert constraints, by dragging one component to another component; also called *drag-mate*.

angular dimension: A dimension used to define the angle between two lines.

arc: A circular curve in which all of the points are an equal distance from the center point.

arrowless dimensioning: A dimensioning method that provides coordinates from established datum's those are usually located at the corner of the part or the axis of a feature. Also called *rectangular coordinate dimensioning without dimension lines* or ordinate dimensioning.

assembly: A grouping of one or more design components.

assembly drawing: A 2D representation of an assembly.

assembly constraints: Constraints that establish geometric relationships and positions between one component face, edge, or axis and another component face, edge, or axis.

auxiliary view: A view used to show the true size and shape of an inclined surface that is not parallel to any of the projected views, including the front, top, bottom, left-side, right-side, and back views.

axis of rotation: The pivot point around which the selected geometry is copied.

B

balloon: A shape, usually circular, that is connected to an assembly component by a leader. It contains an identification number or letter that refers to an item in the parts list.

base environment: The overall working environment, within which secondary environments exist.

base feature: The initial model feature, on which all others are based.

baseline dimensioning: A dimensioning method in which the size and location of features are given in reference to a datum. Also referred to as *datum dimensioning*.

base view: The first view placed in a drawing, to which all other views are added.

bend radius: The inside radius of a formed feature.

bend relief: Relief typically added to a sheet metal part to relieve stress, or the tear, that occurs when a portion of a piece of material is bent.

bent: Formed using a brake, die, mandrel, roller, or similar tools.

border: A rectangle or polygon near the edge of the drawing sheet that defines the usable drawing area of the drawing sheet. Borders may also include zone numbers and center marks.

boundary patch: A surface formed by patching the space within a selected closed region.

bowtie grips: Handlebar endpoints used to adjust the shape of a spline.

browser bar (browser): A panel that displays all the items in the current model or drawing.

C

cascading menu: A secondary menu that contains options related to the chosen menu item.

catalog feature: A feature, part, or assembly stored in a catalog that can be inserted into a part model as a feature.

centerline: A line that defines an axis of symmetry or the center of a circular feature.

center of gravity: The center of model mass, where balance occurs.

center point: The intersection point of the X, Y, and Z axes in 3D space, or 0,0,0.

chamfers: Angled planar faces added to lines or curves. Angled planar faces placed on a feature edge.

child node: Subordinate nodes that create, are associated with, or are consumed by the parent node item.

circular feature pattern: Occurrences of features copied and positioned a specified distance apart around an axis.

circular pattern: An arrangement of copies of a feature around an imaginary circle, a designated number of times, and at a specified distance apart.

circumscribed: Describes a polygon in which the flats are tangent to an imaginary circle; circumscribed polygons are measured across the polygon flats.

closed loop: A sketch that is fully closed and does not contain any gaps or openings.

coil: A spiral, or helix, feature used primarily to create springs, detailed threads, and similar items.

coincident constraint: A constraint that forces two points to share the same location.

combs: Lines added to the spline to help illustrate and analyze the spline curvature.

components: The individual parts and subassemblies used to create an assembly.

composite iMates: Two or more iMates linked together and added to a single component; used for the same assembly operation.

constant fillets and rounds: Fillets and rounds that have a curve radius that does not change.

constraints: Parameters that control the size, location, and position of model elements, including sketches and features. Restrictions applied to sketches to define sketch geometry in reference to other sketch geometry. Also called *geometric constraints*.

construction geometry: Geometry used for construction purposes only. Inventor cannot use construction geometry to build sketched features.

consumed: Used up in the creation of a model or feature.

context-sensitive shortcut menu: Menu in which only items associated with the current work environment and application are available.

control keys: Shortcut key combinations that include the [Ctrl] key and a character key.

coordinate system: The system of XYZ coordinate values that defines the location of points in 3D space.

corner chamfers: Angled faces that replace square corners on sheet metal features.

corner relief: Relief typically added to a sheet metal part to relieve stress at a bend corner at the intersection of two or three faces.

corner rip: A feature that opens closed, usually square, corners.

corner round: A curve placed at an inside or outside sheet metal corner.

corner seams: Features that add or remove material to form a gap at sheet metal part corners. Corner seams create an appropriate corner transition for folding and to allow for unfolding.

counter bored hole: A drilled hole that has a larger-diameter cylindrical opening at the top; typically used when a flush surface is necessary, such as to hide a binding screw head.

countersunk hole: Similar to a counter bored hole, but the recess is tapered, resulting in a conical shape that is often used to hide a screw head.

curve: A straight or bent continuous object, such as a line, arc, spline, or circle.

cut: Remove volume from an existing extrusion by subtracting a new extrusion from it. Any process, such as shearing, punching, or laser, water jet, or similar process, used to remove material.

cutting-plane line: A line that represents the cutting plane of the section, which is the location where the view is sliced to show interior features.

cutting tool: A surface, quilt, 2D sketch curve, work plane or existing feature face intersecting the surface to trim that provides an edge to which the item is trimmed.

D

dangling geometry: A condition that results when additional positioning information is required in order for iFeature insertion to occur; primarily due to issues with the initial iFeature sketch and existing feature geometry.

database: A system that stores every model characteristic, including calculations, sketches, features, dimensions, geometric constraints, when each piece of the model was created, and all other model parameters and properties.

datum: A theoretically exact point, axis, or plane from which the location or geometric characteristics of features originate.

datum dimensioning: A dimensioning method in which the size and location of features are given in reference to a datum. Also referred to as *baseline dimensioning*.

decals: Images applied to a part or assembly to display information or decoratea product.

demote: Group more than one part in an assembly to create a subassembly.

dependents: Assembly component files referenced by the assembly.

dependent views: Views projected from and linked to another view, such as a base view.

derived components: Features that can contain a complete model consisting of several features, or even multiple parts; often used as a base feature. A saved part or assembly that can be inserted in a part as a feature.

design session: Time spent working on a project, including analyzing design parameters and using Inventor.

detail view: A view that shows a small, complex part feature at a larger scale.

dialog box: A window-like part of the user interface that contains various kinds of information and settings.

diameter: The distance across a circle from one side to the other through the center.

diameter dimension: A dimension used to define the diameter of a circle or circular object.

dimension: A measurement that numerically defines the size and location of sketch geometry, such as the length of a line, diameter of a circle, or radius of an arc. Specifications of the size and shape of object features so that parts can be manufactured; along with notes and other text, also specify the location and characteristics of geometry and surface texture.

docked: Describes interface items that are locked into position on an edge of the Inventor window (top, bottom, left, or right).

document units: The units used to define the linear, angular, time, and mass measurements and precision in models and drawings.

double bend: A bend between two parallel faces that are not coplanar.

drag-mate: Establishing assembly constraints, including mate, flush, tangent, and insert constraints, by dragging one component to another component; also called *alt-drag*.

drawing annotation tools: Tools that allow you to create annotations such as dimensions, notes, and other text on drawings.

drawing dimensions: Dimensions added to the drawing using Inventor's drawing annotation tools.

drawing sheet: A representation of the physical limits of the paper size on which the drawing will be printed.

drawings: 2D representations of models containing views, dimensions, and annotations.

drilled hole: The most basic hole type, with no counterbore, spotface, or countersink where the hole begins.

driven: Manipulated to see the amount of movement between components, pause movement, see adaptivity, and detect collisions between components.

driven dimension: A dimension used for reference purposes only. Reference dimensions are enclosed in parentheses to show that they are driven.

E

ellipse: An oval-like shape that contains both a major axis and a minor axis.

embossing: The process of raising shapes or text off the surface of an object that has volume, such as a block; the opposite of engraving.

engraving: The process of cutting into, or impressing, shapes or text into the surface of an object that has volume; the opposite of embossing.

external threads: Thread forms on an external feature such as a pin, shaft, bolt, or screw.

extrusion: A surface or solid that has a fixed cross-sectional profile determined by a sketch profile. The sketch profile is extended (extruded) along a linear path to create the 3D feature or part.

F

face draft: A taper placed on a part surface.

feature pattern: An arrangement of copied existing features, generating occurrences of the features. An arrangement of features in a specific pattern, or configuration; created using feature pattern tools.

fillets: Rounded interior corners; fillets add material to corners. A curve placed at the inside intersection of two or more faces, adding material to a feature.

flat angle: The number of degrees a coil end travels without pitch.

flat end: A type of coil end in which the first or last coil is adjusted to create a flat start or finish for the spring.)

flat pattern: A 2D drawing representing the final, unfolded part.

floating: Describes interface items, displayed within a border, that can be freely resized or moved.

flush solution: A constraint that positions two faces along the same plane, facing the same direction.

flyout: A button that presents additional, related tool buttons, much like a cascading menu.

fly-through: A viewing process that shows how it would look if you could fly in and around the actual product you are modeling.

frequently used subfolder: A virtual folder within a project that stores the paths to folders and files you use frequently.

fully constrained model: A model that has no freedom of movement.

full radius fillets and rounds: Fillets and rounds controlled by the linear dimension of a feature, such as the thickness of a part or width of a slot, producing half of a circle or cylinder; most often associated with a round.

G

general notes: Notes that apply to the entire drawing. General notes are usually placed together in the lower-left or upper-right corner of the drawing or in the title block.

geometric constraints: Restrictions applied to sketches to define sketch geometry in reference to other sketch geometry. Also called *constraints*.

geometric dimensioning and tolerancing (GD&T): The dimensioning and tolerancing of individual features of a part where the permissible variations relate to characteristics of form, profile, orientation, runout, or the location of features.

grab bars: Two thin bars at the top or left edge of a docked or floating item; used to move the item.

graphical user interface (GUI): On-screen interface items.

grounded component: An assembly component that is fixed in position, has no freedom of movement, and cannot be driven.

grounded work point: A work point completely fixed to an X, Y, Z coordinate at which it is placed.

guide rail: A 2D or 3D sketched curve that is used with the sweep path to manipulate and further control the shape of a sweep.

guide surface: A surface that helps control

the shape of a sweep along a complex path.

H

height: In a coil, the total depth of the coil from the center of the starting profile to the center of the ending profile.

help string: A short description of what happens if you select a tool or option over which the cursor is hovering, or if a tool is selected, a prompt indicating the appropriate action is shown.

hem: Flanges used to add strength to or relieve the sharpness of exposed edges, or to connect separate edges or parts together.

hot keys: Single character keys on the keyboard that allow you to access certain predefined tools.

I

icon: A small graphic representing an application, file, or tool.

i-drop: The process of dragging and dropping shared content into component files, or the tool used for this process.

iFeature: An existing feature or set of features you create and then save and store in a catalog to be used in other models. A stored feature that can be inserted in a part as a feature.

iMates: Constraints placed on an individual component that are later used for assembly.

included angle: The angle between two selected edges, curves, axes, faces, planes, or a combination of objects, such as an edge and a face.

included file: A separate project file linked to the current project.

increment: A set amount by which values increase in equal steps. For example, with an increment of 2, a size would increase to 4, 6, 8, 10, and so on.

inferred: Automatically detected using logic.

inscribed: Describes a polygon in which the corners touch an imaginary circle; inscribed polygons are measured from the corners.

interface: The tools and techniques used to provide information to and receive information from a computer application. Also called a *user interface*.

internal threads: Thread forms on an internal hole feature.

iProperties: Inventor file properties used to define a variety of file and design characteristics.

isometric view: A 3D view in which all three axes are shown at equal angles (120°) with the plane of projection.

J

join: Combine two or more existing features to create a single feature.

K

k-factor: A multiple, typically between .25 and .5, that locates the neutral axis.

L

leader: A line that connects the beginning or end of a note to the feature it describes. Leaders usually have a horizontal shoulder on the end nearest the text. The other end has an arrow pointing to the feature.

left-hand threads: Threads that move a left-hand threaded bolt forward in a counterclockwise direction.

library: A folder that contains files used in a project or several different projects.

library search paths: The locations in which Inventor looks for library files on the computer's hard drive or on the network.

linear dimension: A type of dimension used to define the vertical and horizontal size and location of object features.

local notes: Notes that apply to a specific feature or features on the drawing. Also called *specific notes*.

loft: A feature that references and blends two or more sections located on different planes.

loft centerline: A rail that acts as a path for blending sections along and symmetrically around the centerline sketch.

lump: Any set of external feature or surface faces created when you develop a solid model.

M

mate solution: A constraint that places two faces along the same plane facing in opposite directions, two axes collinear to each other, two edges collinear to each other, or two points matched together.

mirrored feature: mirrored features: A mirror image of an existing feature created symmetrically over a specified plane.

mirror plane: A plane of symmetry about which features are mirrored.

miter gap: Space between faces created during a corner seam or miter operation.

model dimensions: Dimensions that were used to create and constrain the model from which drawing content has been extracted.

modeling failure: The result of conflicting constraints that are impossible to apply to the model.

model parameters: Parameters that relate to the model. Model parameters are added when you insert a model view or add model information, such as dimensions.

model space: A space, or environment, in which the model defines the display orientation, regardless of the position of the model in the graphics window; the center is associated with the model pivot point.

monodetail drawing: A drawing of a single part on one sheet.

motion constraints: Assembly constraints that identify how movable components should move in reference to other movable components, using a specified ratio and direction.

multidetail drawing: A drawing of several parts on one sheet.

multiple document interface: An interface that allows you to have several documents or document views open at the same time. Also called *multiple design interface*.

N

natural end: A type of coil end that occurs as the natural result of the pitch, revolution, height, and profile of the coil.

network: Several ribs or webs created using the same direction and thickness.

neutral axis: The axis of a bend radius where neither stretching nor compressing occurs.

nominal size: The designated size of a commercial product.

nominal value: The value of a commercial product; intended to be the true drawn size without any specified limits.

O

oblique view: A 3D view in which the plane of projection is parallel to the front surface, and a receding angle is applied.

offset: Form objects parallel to the specified geometry at a specified distance apart. When referring to the

Thicken/Offset
tool, the process of offsetting a surface from a face or surface, similar to offsetting a work plane from a face. When referring to threads, the distance from the edge of the face to the beginning of threads.

open loop: A sketch that includes a gap(s) between objects.

open sketch profile: A sketch profile that does not form a closed loop.

ordinate dimensioning: A dimensioning method that provides coordinates from established datums that are usually located at the corner of the part or the axis of a feature. Also called *rectangular coordinate dimensioning without dimension lines* or *arrowless dimensioning*.

origin: The center point (0,0,0) of the model's XYZ coordinate system.

orphaned annotations: Annotations that have been moved away from a drawing view associated with model geometry.

orthographic view: A 2D view, or projection, in which the line of sight is perpendicular to a surface, such as the front of an object or the XY plane.

over-constrained model: A model with too many constraints.

P

pan: Reposition the display of objects in the graphics window.

panel bar: A panel-like window that appears by default on the left side of the Inventor graphics window. Panel bars are the primary default location for accessing design tools.

parallel: A geometric construction that specifies that objects such as lines and ellipse axes will never intersect, no matter how long they become.

parameters: Characteristics that control the size, shape, and position of model geometry. Shape and size limits placed on sketches and features.

parametric solid modeling: A form of modeling in which parameters and constraints drive the model form and function to produce models that contain object volume and mass data that can be used to analyze internal and external object characteristics.

parent node: An item in the tree structure, similar to a folder, that is associated with subordinate child nodes.

part: An item or product or an element of an assembly.

partial auxiliary view: An auxiliary view that shows the true size and shape of only the inclined surface, eliminating any projected geometry that may be foreshortened.

parts list: A table that records and displays the parts and subassemblies used to create an assembly.

path: A guide, or route, for creating sketched features.

pattern occurrences: Representations of patterned features that identify how many features are present because of the pattern operation.

perpendicular: A geometric construction that defines a 90° angle between objects such as lines and ellipse axes.

pitch: The distance parallel to the axis between a point on one coil spiral to the corresponding point on the next coil spiral. (Ch. 5) The distance parallel to the axis from a point on one thread to the corresponding point on the next thread.

pivot point: The point that acts as the center point when you are viewing and rotating model space objects.

placed features: Features added to an existing feature without using a sketch.

placed sections: Loft sections that are created without a sketch and are placed along a selected centerline. Placed sections are calculated based on the loft cross section at the selected location.

profile: The side or section outline of a sketched feature.

projects: Files that manage and organize folders and files for specific design jobs.

promote: Add to the part environment. Remove parts from a subassembly and make them individual parts in the parent assembly.

pull direction: The direction in which the casting mold is pulled or removed from the part.

pull-down menus: A text-based menu input system in which menu items appear when you pick the menu name.

punch: A press or similar tool used to form a specific shape or hole in sheet metal. Also called a *sheet metal punch*.

Q

quilt: A set of combined surfaces.

R

radius: The distance from the center of a circle or arc to its circumference.

radius dimension: A dimension used to define the radius of an arc or circular feature.

rail: A 2D or 3D sketched curve that is used in conjunction with sections to manipulate and further control the loft shape.

read-only: A file open option that allows you to view a file, but not make changes to it.

realtime zooming: Zooming that can be viewed as it is performed.

rectangular coordinate dimensioning without dimension lines: A dimensioning method that provides coordinates from established datums that are usually located at the corner of the part or the axis of a feature. Also called *ordinate dimensioning* or *arrowless dimensioning*.

rectangular feature pattern: Occurrences of features copied and positioned a specified distance apart, in rows and columns.

rectangular pattern: An arrangement of copies of a feature into a designated number of rows and columns placed a specified distance apart.

regular polygon: A geometric shape with three or more sides, such as a triangle, square, or hexagon, with all sides being equal in length and symmetrical about a common center.

revision table: A table that records drawing changes; usually placed in the upper-right corner of the drawing. Also called a *revision* *history block* or *revision block*.

revision tag: A symbol that identifies the location at which the engineering change occurs. The tag corresponds to a specific entry in the revision table. Also called a *revision symbol*.

revolution: A feature created in a circular path around an axis; also called a *revolved feature*. In a coil, one complete spiral, or 360° loop.

revolved feature: A feature created in a circular path around an axis. Also known as a *revolution*.

rib: A closed section of material usually added to reinforce a part without adding excessive material or weight.

right-hand threads: Threads that move a right-hand threaded bolt forward in a clockwise direction

rounds: Rounded exterior corners; rounds remove material from corners. A curve placed on the exterior intersection of two or more faces, removing material from a feature.

S

scale factor: The amount of enlargement or reduction.

screen space: A space, or environment, in which the graphics window controls model display; the center is located at the center of the graphics window.

sculpt: The process of using intersecting surfaces to add or remove solid mass.

sections: Sketches and existing feature faces used to develop loft features. A view that splits a part along a cutting-plane line to expose the interior features of the part. Also called a *section view*.

section view: A view that splits a part along a cutting-plane line to expose the interior features of the part. Also called a *section*.

setback: Point at which a fillet or round on one edge begins to combine with a fillet or round of at least two other edges.

shared content: Files available on the Internet, such as bolts from a bolt manufacturer, or components accessible on an intranet system, such as standard parts that are used for developing assemblies. Also called *third-party content*.

sharing: Making a sketch available for additional features after it has been used to create a feature.

sheet formats: Predefined, multiview drawing sheet templates that contain a default border and title block for various standard sheet sizes.

sheet metal punch: A press or similar tool used to form a specific shape or hole in sheet metal. Also called a *punch*.

shell: An operation that removes material from a feature and creates a hollow space or opening.

shortcut keys: Keyboard key combinations that allow you to access predefined tools.

shortcut menus: Menus that allow access to tools and options by right-clicking anywhere in the graphics window or on an object or selection.

sketch: A 2D drawing that provides the profile and/or guide for developing a sketched feature.

sketch center points: Points used to define the location of center points for features that reference center points, such as holes and sheet metal punches.

sketched features: Features such as extrusions, revolutions, sweeps, lofts, and coils that are built from a sketch.

sketch helix: A winding spiral shape primarily used to create springs, detailed threads, and similar items.

sketch pattern: Multiple arranged copies, or a pattern, of sketch shapes.

sketch points: Points used for construction purposes to help you develop sketch geometry.

spacing: In patterning, the distance between occurrences based on the width of the selected features and the distance between
the copies.

specific notes: Notes that apply to a specific feature or features on the drawing. Also called *local notes*.

spline: A complex curve defined by control points along the curve.

split: A feature that removes a portion of a model or divides faces at a separation sketch or plane.

spotface: Similar to a counterbore, but shallower; typically applied when a flush surface is necessary, such as to hide a flat washer, or in casting applications.

standard: A set of styles and other general drawing preferences that has been agreed upon and recommended for use by an industry, government, military, or standardssetting organization.

steering wheels: Circular navigation tools that allow you to navigate around a model.

stitched: Two or more surfaces combined to form a single surface or quilt. supplement)

style library: A folder, Design Data by default, that houses styles in XML file format.

subassembly: An assembly placed in a larger assembly, such as switch, or spring assembly; subassemblies may be used more than once in the final assembled product.

surface extrusion: A volume less shape that is primarily used for construction purposes, allowing you to generate advanced models.

surface finish: The allowable roughness, waviness, lay, and flaws on a surface.

sweep: A feature created by guiding, or sweeping, a sketch profile along a sketch path.

T

table-driven iFeature: An iFeature that allows you to create multiple variations of the original iFeature using information stored in a spreadsheet.

tabular dimensioning: A type of arrowless dimensioning in which coordinate dimensions and size dimensions are given in a table that correlates with features on the drawing with a hole tag.

tangent constraint: A geometric construction that specifies how a curve touches another curve at the point of tangency.

tap: Use a machine tool to form an interior thread.

tapered threads: Threads often used for pipe fittings when a liquid or airtight seal is required.

templates: Files with predefined settings used to begin new documents.

thickening: The process of adding a solid to a face or surface, similar to a solid extrusion.

third-party content: Files available on the Internet, such as bolts from a bolt manufacturer, or components accessible on an intranet system, such as standard parts that are used for developing assemblies. Also called *shared content*.

thread class: The designated amount, or grade, of tolerance specified for the thread, ranging from fine to coarse threads.

threads: Grooves cut in a spiral fashion in or around the face of a cylindrical or conical feature.

title block: An area on the drawing sheet that contains information about the model, company, drafter, tolerances, and other design information.

tolerance stack: Text that is stacked horizontally without a fraction bar.

tool buttons: Buttons in a toolbar, each with a specific icon, that activate a tool or option.

tooltip: A small text box that displays when you hover over a button, giving information about the function of the button.

trails: Connection graphics between components that show their relative positions in the assembly.

transitional constraints: Constraints that identify relationships between the transitioning path of a fixed component and a component moving along the path.

transition angle: The number of degrees a coil end travels, or transitions, with pitch.

tweaks: Component modifications made during the preparation of a presentation.

U

under-constrained model: A model with elements that are unclear, can be changed or moved, or remain undefined.

user interface: The tools and techniques used to provide information to and receive information from a computer application. Also called an *interface*.

user parameters: Additional parameters defined by the user.

V

variable fillets and rounds: Fillets and rounds that have different curved radii placed at precise points between the start and end of a feature edge.

vertex: When referring to filet and round setbacks, the intersection of three or more edges.

virtual component: An assembly component used primarily to define a separate bill of materials item, without creating a model.

void: Any set of internal feature faces that define a hollow area in a solid.

W

walk-through: A viewing process that shows how it would look if you could walk in and around the actual product you are modeling.

web: An open section of material usually added to reinforce a part without adding excessive material or weight.

wedges: The parts of a steering wheel that contain navigation tools.

weldment: An assembly in which parts are fixed together with welds.

wireframe model: A model that contains only information about model edges and the intersection of edges.

wireframe representation: A display in which surfaces are removed so that you can see the edges clearly.

work axis: An axis used to create construction lines and axes. A parametric reference line that can be located anywhere in space.

work features: Features that direct the location and arrangement of other features. Construction points, lines, and surfaces that create reference elements anywhere in space to help position and generate additional features.

work planes: Planes that are used to create construction planes. Flat reference surfaces that can be located anywhere in space.

work points: Points used to create construction points. Parametric reference points that can be located on any part feature or in 3D space.

workspace: The default folder where files are located in a project.

Z

zoom in: Increase the displayed size of objects in the graphics window to view a smaller portion of the model, but in greater detail.

zoom out: Reduce the displayed size of objects in the graphics window to display more of the model, but in view less detail.

www.ingramcontent.com/pod-product-compliance
Lightning Source LLC
Chambersburg PA
CBHW081815300426
44116CB00014B/2368